Economics and Power

In the economic debate, power is defined and studied mainly as an interpersonal relation occurring out of perfect competition. This is a consequence of the combination of methodological individualism and the assumption of competition as a natural and everlasting coordinating mechanism, operating without any sort of coercion. This methodology, however, is not adequate to analyse the forms of social coercion that characterise capitalism.

Economics and Power criticises the main theories of power developed in economic literature, analysing ultraliberal contractualism to radical political economics, and ultimately suggesting a Marxist conception of power and coercion in capitalism. Palermo's ontological argument is rooted in the philosophy of 'critical realism'. This unique volume presents his main finding as being that the essential coercive mechanism of capitalism is indeed competition. Capitalist power is not caused by a lack of competition, but by the central role it plays in this mode of production. Following this, the chapters reconstruct a Marxian conception of power where it is analysed as a social relation and argues that perfect competition does in fact exist under the disguise of capitalist power. This book criticises the construct of power and the underlying ideas surrounding perfect competition.

This book will be of interest to those who study political economy, as well as economic theory and philosophy.

Giulio Palermo is Researcher in Economics at the University of Brescia, Italy.

Routledge Frontiers of Political Economy

For a complete list of titles in this series please visit www.routledge.com/
books/series/SE0345

Economics and Power
A Marxist critique

Giulio Palermo

Routledge
Taylor & Francis Group

LONDON AND NEW YORK

First published 2016 by Routledge

2 Park Square, Milton Park, Abingdon, Oxfordshire OX14 4RN

52 Vanderbilt Avenue, New York, NY 10017

Routledge is an imprint of the Taylor & Francis Group, an informa business

First issued in paperback 2019

British Library Cataloguing in Publication Data

A catalogue record for this book is available from the British Library

Library of Congress Cataloging in Publication Data

Names: Palermo, Giulio, author.

Title: Economics and power : a Marxist critique / Giulio Palermo.

Description: Abingdon, Oxon ; New York, NY : Routledge, 2016.

Identifiers: LCCN 2015049336| ISBN 9781138923096 (hardback) | ISBN 9781315685335 (ebook)

Subjects: LCSH: Marxian economics. | Economics--Philosophy. | Power (Social sciences)

Classification: LCC HB97.5 .P247 2016 | DDC 335.4/12--dc23

LC record available at http://lccn.loc.gov/2015049336

ISBN: 978-1-138-92309-6 (hbk)

ISBN: 978-0-367-25093-5 (pbk)

Typeset in Times New Roman

by Saxon Graphics Ltd, Derby

Contents

Illustrations

Figures

Tables

Preface and acknowledgements

This book is the result of a long period of research on power and the 'new right', initiated with my doctoral thesis in economics, defended in 1997.[1] Since then, I have developed my critique in different directions and this book reorders these past arguments into an organic work.

In these years, the attempt to behave coherently with my critique and to address the latter against the university as well – against its power-based mechanisms and against its social and economic role in the capitalist system – has caused me an unpleasant isolation, censorship and repression from academic hierarchies.[2] This is why I have no acknowledgement to address within the academia.

Naturally, my ideas have been influenced by the academic debates of our time and my work has benefited from the comments and criticisms of many authors. But the academy is only one side of the coin: the other is society. No academician can develop a critical conception of power without being part of a movement fighting against power. Rather than mentioning the professors and researchers that have most influenced me, I prefer thus to remember all the comrades that continue the struggle against the coercive conditions of this society and fight to free critical thinking from the power mechanisms that imprison it. It is to the anti-capitalist movement, in all its forms and developments, that I dedicate my work.

Having used ample parts of articles that I have published, I thank the *Cambridge Journal of Economics*, *Capital and Class*, the *Journal of Economic Issues*, the *Journal of Economic Methodology* and *Science and Society* for having given me the free right to use the following articles:

Ankarloo, Daniel and Giulio Palermo (2004), Anti-Williamson: A Marxian critique of new institutional economics, *Cambridge Journal of Economics*, vol. 28, n. 3, pp. 413–29.

Palermo, Giulio (1999), The convergence of Austrian economics and new institutional economics: Methodological inconsistencies and political motivations, *Journal of Economic Issues*, vol. 33, n. 2, pp. 277–85.

——(2000), Economic power and the firm in new institutional economics: Two conflicting problems, *Journal of Economic Issues*, vol. 34, n. 3, pp. 573–601.

——(2007A), Misconceptions of power: From Alchian and Demsetz to Bowles and Gintis, *Capital and Class*, vol. 92, pp. 147–85.

——(2007B), The ontology of economic power in capitalism: Mainstream economics and Marx, *Cambridge Journal of Economics*, vol. 31, n. 4, pp. 539–61.

——(2014), The economic debate on power: A Marxist critique, *Journal of Economic Methodology*, vol. 21, n. 2, pp. 175–92.

——(2016A), Power, competition and the free trader vulgaris', *Cambridge Journal of Economics*, vol. 40, n. 1, pp. 259–81.

——(2016B), Post Walrasian economics: A Marxist critique, *Science and Society*, vol. 80, n. 3, pp. 346–74.

Notes

1 *Coordinamento, competizione e potere economico: I limiti teorici della 'nuova destra' nell'analisi dei rapporti tra stato, impresa e mercato*, PhD thesis, University of Rome 'La Sapienza'.

2 Beside my involvement in political struggles, within and outside the university, I have criticised the role of power in the Italian university system in some articles published in Italian political journals and in two books: 1) *L'università dei baroni: Centocinquant'anni di storia tra cooptazione, contestazione e mercificazione*, Milano: Punto Rosso, 2011; and 2) *Baroni e portaborse: I rapporti di potere nell'università*, Roma: Editori International Riuniti, 2012.

Abbreviations

DMC Decision making context
OS   Organisational structure
POS Power over somebody
PTA Power to act

1   Introduction

This book is about the role of power in capitalism and in economic theory. In both cases, power is strictly related to competition. By following Marx, I argue that, in real capitalism, competition is the main coercing mechanism through which capital asserts its laws. It imposes the needs of capital over society, governs the reproduction of social classes and regulates the balance of power in interpersonal relations. The specificity of capitalism with respect to other modes of production is that power relations emerge and evolve under the laws of competition. Competition is thus one of the keys to understanding capitalist power.

In mainstream economic theory, power is also linked to competition but, curiously, for quite the opposite reason. Neoclassical economics and its 'heterodox' developments conceive of power as the negation of perfect competition: in the reign of perfect competition, they maintain, nobody has power over anybody else. Therefore, they do not look at competition to understand what power *is* but to define what it *is not*. Anyway, willy-nilly, competition is at the core of this conception of power as well, even if only as a negative benchmark.

In one case, power depends on competition 'positively', because in capitalism competition is itself a mechanism of coercion and because it regulates power dynamics in interpersonal relations. In the other, it depends on competition 'negatively', because, as a matter of definition, the latter is conceived of as the standard of power-free relations. Before defining my strategy to approach the study of power, two things are then already clear: first, a Marxist approach to capitalist power cannot abstract from the coercing role that competition assumes in this mode of production; second, a systematic critique of the neoclassical conception of power is inevitably also a critique of the notion of competition implicit in this conception. This is why a book on power in capitalism and in economics is inevitably also a book on competition.

The discussion of this apparent paradox – the fact that, to understand power, competition is essential because of its existence, in one case, and because of its non-existence, in the other – is the main theme of this book. My scientific goal is twofold: first, to understand the relationship between power and competition, not merely in abstract terms, but in the capitalist mode of production; second, to explain why this relationship appears as a dichotomy in neoclassical economics. In the same way as Marx explained the essence of capitalist exploitation behind the appearances of competition and equal exchange, my project is to explain the essence of capitalist power behind the appearances of competition and free interactions. My thesis is that *power and competition are not really antagonistic in capitalism, but express rather the essence and the appearance of capital in this mode of production.*

Like all modes of production, capitalism has its specific mechanisms of working and reproduction, which impose various forms of coercion and power on social and interpersonal relations. As we will see, in capitalism, the main mechanism that govern the reproduction process is competition. Competition is therefore also responsible for the specific forms of power and coercion of this mode of production. The problem is that capitalism is a mystified system, in which the appearance of individual freedom in interpersonal relations tends to obfuscate the exploitative nature of class relations. Competition is the vehicle of this contradiction between appearances and essence. Therefore, in a Marxist perspective, it is not an abstract analysis of competition, but a critique of its role in capitalism, that allows explaining both its apparent power-free content and its essential coercing nature.

The representation of power as the negation of competition is instead a consequence of the pretence of universality of neoclassical economics, which leads to approach even the issue of power in abstract, a-historical, terms. Its relations with the reproducing mechanisms of capitalism are not investigated simply because neoclassical economics does not characterise capitalism as a historical mode of production – which reproduces itself through particular mechanisms, developing under particular historical conditions – but as a set of economic laws that have always existed and will exist forever. The first of these universal laws is competition. Competition, in neoclassical economics, is the *deus ex machina* of economic phenomena, a universal cause that explains everything, but cannot be explained, a natural condition based on individual freedom and spontaneous interaction. This is why, logically, power can only be introduced as an exception to this universal power-free notion and this is why, more generally, there can be no distinction between essence and appearance in this conception.

The main problem in my attempt to develop a Marxist conception of power and competition, is that, unlike competition, power is not a pivotal category in Marx's work. Marx does not focus directly on the power content of interpersonal relations but on capital. His idea is that, in the capitalist mode of production, the laws of capital accumulation define the laws of social interaction. It is thus meaningless to approach the problem of power before having explained these social laws. Competition is part of these social laws. If power is not in the forefront in Marx's work, it is because logically this issue can be approached only after the critique of capital and competition.

Of course, the modern neoclassical approach to power does not follow Marx's method. Rather, it develops its conception of power from the mystified conception of perfect competition of old neoclassical economics. My critique of this approach is thus nothing else but an attempt at demystifying this conception of power by developing Marx's critique of capital and by showing the forms of coercion that capital imposes on social relations.

But the best way to move from a critical to a constructive perspective and develop an organic conception of power and coercion from Marx's analysis is not by focusing directly on power, but by developing his critique of competition. Only after having fully understood the coercive nature of competition in this mode of production can we explain rigorously the different levels at which coercion and power affect social and interpersonal relations.

In the next sections, I begin by introducing the debate on power in social sciences. This debate has developed around a general controversy between 'elitists' and 'democratic pluralists', with the former contending that, in capitalism, power is concentrated in the hands of a tiny circle of subjects, and the latter suggesting instead that it is widespread in society, without significant asymmetries.

Then, I focus on economics. With respect to other social sciences, the economics debate is 'flat', in the sense that it neglects many of the problematic dimensions of power discussed in sociology and political science. The theoretical contribution of neoclassical economics consists mainly in associating perfect competition to power-free relations, thereby transforming the controversy about the role and the concentration of power in society into a controversy about the spread of perfect competition in the economy, with liberal economists seeing competition everywhere and radicals considering it a rare exception in the real world. These apparently opposite positions, however, converge on the same idea that power relations develop only when perfect competition is impossible.

After this introduction to the academic debate, I discuss some methodological and ontological issues, which are at the basis of both my critique and my proposal. First, I focus on the choice of the explanatory categories of power. I argue that, in neoclassical economics, these categories are not derived from an analysis of the essential relations of the capitalist mode of production, but are simply assumed as a by-product of methodological individualism, the only rigorous methodology according to this economic school. Marx's critique follows instead a different logic. Explaining categories and methodological choices are explicitly grounded on ontological arguments. His critique of capital is not the result of a convenient methodology, but the development of an ontological inquiry into the essential categories of capitalism. The commodity, value, money, social classes and all more complex categories of this mode of production are not introduced as abstract, methodologically convenient, notions, but as necessary entities of the capitalist ontology.

Next, I discuss the role of these categories within historical materialism. I analyse, in particular, the causal nexus between class relations, exploitation, social coercion and interpersonal powers. I show that, in a historical materialist perspective, social coercion and interpersonal powers develop together and reinforce each other. Logically, however, the existence of social coercion in capitalism does not depend on interpersonal powers, but on social classes.

Finally, with these methodological and ontological premises, I articulate my strategy to demystify the neoclassical approach and to elaborate an alternative conception of capitalist power, starting from Marx's critique of capital and competition.

In the last section, I present the structure of the book.

The dimensions of power in social sciences

The subject of power has been investigated mainly within sociology and political science. At the roots of these investigations, there is Max Weber's (1968, vol. 1, p. 53) definition of power as 'the probability that one actor within a social relationship will be in a position to carry out his own will despite resistance'.[1] In the academic debate, this definition has been applied mainly to the study of situations in which an actor is able to get his/her way in social decisions when others are openly opposed.[2]

The debate is opened by the works of Floyd Hunter (1953), Wright Mills (1956) and Elmer Schattschneider (1960) who argue that, in the United states, power is asymmetrically distributed and concentrated. This thesis has provoked the harsh reactions of Robert Dahl (1961) and Nelson Polsby (1963), who have developed some empirical analyses and have concluded that in the American society power is spread pluralistically. These contrasting positions, however, are, to a large extent, the fruit of different theoretical frameworks by which these authors have made Weber's definition operational. In Dahl's framework, for instance, the exercise of power presupposes that two or more groups have conflicting preferences and that they manifest this explicitly. Out of these conditions, the author assumes that there is no room for the exercise of power.

In his little and influential book, Steven Lukes (1974) argues that this is a restrictive conception of power that can be called 'one-dimensional', and identifies two other views of power: the two-dimensional one, developed by Peter Bachrach and Morton Baratz (1962, 1963, 1970), and his own radical, or three-dimensional, view.[3]

Bachrach and Baratz's (1962) second dimension of power – which they call it the second 'face' of power – consists in the ability to condition the issues that are the object of collective decision. If *A* manages to confine the scope of decision making to particular issues and prevents *B* from bringing to the fore issues that might be detrimental to his/her own preferences, *A* is actually exercising power over *B*. The control of the agenda, in this broader theoretical framework, is actually a form of power. This casts doubts on the general validity of the democratic pluralism thesis.[4]

This two-dimensional view, however, is still inadequate for Lukes. The political agenda, he argues, is not necessarily controlled by the intentional action of particular individuals; it depends also on collective action and on the form of organisation of the system ('systemic effect'). Moreover, the notion of power should not be restricted to observable conflicts, because power over an individual may also be exercised by influencing, shaping or determining his/her very wants. Within this framework, even the absence of grievance does not imply genuine consensus, since those who are subject to power might not be able to express their *real* interests and might even be unaware of them. And most importantly, there might exist forms of coercion on individual choice that depend on the overall structure of the decision making system and that cannot be ascribed to the action of any single individual.

Besides these conceptions of power as an interpersonal relation, Lukes (1974, pp. 31–7) criticises the conceptions elaborated by Talcott Parsons (1957, 1963A, 1963B) and Hannah Arendt (1970), by noticing that:

> They focus on the locution 'power to', ignoring 'power over'. Thus power indicates a 'capacity', a 'facility', an 'ability', not a relationship. Accordingly, the conflictual aspect of power – the fact that it is exercised over people – disappears altogether from view.
>
> (Lukes 1974, p. 34)

Lukes also maintains that everything that can be said by means of the notion of 'power to' can be said with greater clarity by means of his own conceptual scheme based on 'power over'.

Although my analysis of economic power is an attempt to develop Lukes' three-dimensional view, I do not think that the point is to establish whether the *relational* notion of power ('power over somebody') is more or less general than the *dispositional* one ('power to act'). The issue is rather to clarify the relations between them and, above all, the way both of them are governed by non-observable structures and mechanisms. In fact, I believe that this is the only way to study 'systemic effects', which Lukes himself regards as an essential aspect of his radical view.

The problem, of course, is to specify correctly what are the systemic effects that govern capitalistic power relations. Different from other approaches, which seek them in morality, justice or democracy, I look at the economy, because it is in the economy that the process of capitalist exploitation imposes the essential forms of power and coercion of capitalism. In my interpretation of Marx, the mechanisms than govern capitalist production and reproduction are also the mechanisms that constrain social development, delimits free action, and impose the imprint of capital in interpersonal relations. It is therefore from the critique of capitalist production and reproduction that I develop a Marxist conception of power in capitalism. This is not to say that the cultural, political, moral or religious spheres have nothing to do with power. On the contrary, it is a claim that, in order to understand the coercive role of the superstructure in its different historical configurations, we must first explain the general forms of capitalist power as they emanate from the essential relation of exploitation that characterises this mode of production.

In my view, it is this lack of critique of the economic base of capitalism that leads even a critical author like Lukes (1985) to counterpose power and 'genuine freedom' and to characterise the formal freedoms of bourgeois democracies as genuine freedoms. Lukes has in fact a critical view on historical materialism. Soon after the introduction of the systemic effect as an essential ingredient of his three-dimensional view, the author quotes Marx's historical materialist conception (Lukes 1974, p. 26). When he develops his own conception of power in capitalism, however, he puts historical materialism aside. Rather than following Marx in his work of demystification of free exchange and competition, Lukes (1985, 2005) develops a conception of power and freedom that simply denies any specific role to the base of capitalism.

As he summarises in the entry on 'emancipation' for the *Dictionary of Marxist thought* (Bottomore 1983), Marx and his followers, especially since Lenin, did not grasp the role of formal freedom in bourgeois democracies and tended to deny the possibility of genuine freedom in capitalism: 'Marx ... wrote of free competition as limited freedom because based on the rule of capital and "therefore *[sic]* at the same time the most complete suspension of all individual freedom" *(Grundrisse*, Notebook VI, Penguin edn, p. 652) ... Such formulations are theoretically in error and have been practically disastrous' (Lukes 1983, p. 173).

This severe conclusion, however, is only a consequence of Lukes' peculiar way of specifying systemic effects in his own conception of power. Theoretically, he downplays the role of the economy and, more generally, questions historical materialism and the logical distinction between the base and the superstructure (Lukes 1982). Power appears thus to be linked to all dimensions of social life – culture, moral, law, politics – without any clear priority among them. The economic base becomes only one of the many possible sources of power and its specific exploitative nature becomes simply irrelevant. In this conception, one can legitimately seek the conditions of compatibility between competition and genuine freedom. But this is simply to assume that competition involves no form of coercion in the capitalist economy and that eventually the problem is in the political, juridical or cultural sphere, like in the mystified conception of bourgeois economics.

The democratisation of capitalism and the development of emancipating processes within this mode of production – the motivations of most critical theorists of power – are decisive scientific questions and urgent political challenges. But these processes can be developed coherently only after having understood the economic forms of coercion of this mode of production and the illusions created by competition. This is the main theoretical shortcoming of the modern approach to power, even in its most advanced and radical expressions, and this is the gap I intend to fill.

But now we must discuss how economists, although better placed to focus on the coercing role of the capitalist economy, have eluded these questions and, in fact, have remained attached to the one-dimensional view of power, without any consideration for the critical debate developed in social sciences.

The unidimensional view of power in economics

In the economics literature, the debate on power has developed mainly as a sub-problem of explaining 'the nature of the firm'. Ronald Coase (1937) formulated this problem by asking the questions: Why do hierarchies exist? What is the coordinating mechanism within the firm? Of course, these questions can be approached in many ways. The acceptance of deductivism, however, and, in particular, of methodological individualism, poses serious restrictions that make the one-dimensional view largely dominant even within important parts of economic heterodoxy. Meta-theoretically speaking, even those parts of Marxism committed to methodological individualism – such as rational choice Marxism and parts of the radical school – develop in fact the same one-dimensional view and are indistinguishable from mainstream neoclassical economics.

This one-dimensional view includes traditional neoclassical economics, with its analysis of market power, the contractual approach of Armen Alchian and Harold Demsetz, the transaction cost economics of Coase and Oliver Williamson, the property right approach of Oliver Hart and John Moore, and those parts of the institutional perspective and of the radical school that accept methodological individualism even if only as a theoretical challenge, personified by authors such as Victor Goldberg and Samuel Bowles and Herbert Gintis.

If I assemble theories that are often considered as competing with one another, it is because their individualist methodology presupposes the same ontology. Ontologically, these theories assume that reality coincides with what is empirically detectable. Methodologically, they seek (what they consider to be) explanations by reducing empirical phenomena to the smallest units of the system, which are assumed to be independent of one another and of the system of which they are part. These units are rational economic agents. Although this approach focuses on the relationship between the capitalist and the worker, these two figures are not *bona fide* social entities. In this ontology, capitalists and workers are simply individuals. Therefore, their eventual power relation within the firm is not found in the capital–labour relation, but in their innate qualities of individuals and in the features of the context in which they interact.

New Institutionalism, for instance, explains the origin of hierarchies in capitalism by assuming that they emerged spontaneously from the interaction of imperfect individuals in an imperfect context. Williamson (1975, p. 21) starts with the assumption that 'in the beginning there were markets' and, by means of comparative statics exercises, *deduces* the emergence of hierarchies as solutions to market failures. His 'explanation' is based on the assumption that individuals have heterogeneous natural endowments, such as 'unequally distributed administrative talent', 'oratorical gifts', 'information processing', and 'decision making skills' (Williamson 1975, pp. 47–52) and that they interact in a context characterised by uncertainty and imperfect information.

The statement that capitalist hierarchies originated without coercion, however, is not documented historically, but argued deductively. The problem for Williamson is not to investigate what has effectively taken place, but to find the conditions that make one institution superior to another, with the (unjustified) assumption that efficiency is always automatically selected. In this conception, hierarchies can exist only where the conditions for perfect competition do not hold. Only in this case can (inborn) individual asymmetries produce direct power relations between individuals.

This conception is common to the whole of the approach to power based on methodological individualism. In a perfectly competitive context, interpersonal relations are assumed to involve no power, and the cause of power relations is found in the empirical conditions that make perfect competition impossible.[5]

Theoretically, perfect competition presupposes full rationality, perfect information, and absence of radical uncertainty and historical time. Therefore, according to this approach, power relations can exist only out of these 'perfect' conditions. Empirically, they must be sought in interpersonal relations characterised by some sort of *imperfection* in the decision making context. Imperfections are thus the true cause of power, in capitalism and in any other mode of production and exchange. Each theorist of power, within this approach, is free to regard at them as the norm or as empirical rarities. But, they all agree that without imperfections there is no power relation.

Methodological choices and ontological necessities

Logically, the choice of the categories that might explain the nature of power relations is the initial problem of any approach to power. In the debate on power, however, this problem is not really discussed. Rather abstract individuals and the abstract decision making contexts in which they are supposed to interact are introduced as simple consequences of methodological individualism and the latter is assumed a-critically, as *the* method of economic theory, without any ontological defence.

Explaining categories, however, cannot be chosen simply for methodological convenience. First we must discover the 'essential' ontological entities of capitalism, those that are necessary for the reproduction of the system. These entities exist because, logically, the system is grounded on them, it reproduces itself through their action. Private property, social classes, capital, competition are not conventional aggregates or abstract notions. They express real entities of capitalism, whose existence is not merely assumed, but proven by the necessary role they play in this mode of production.

Consider class relations. Their central role in Marx's critique is not the result of an *a priori* methodological choice, but the consequence of a simple ontological argument: without buyers and sellers of labour power, capitalism could not reproduce itself. The scientific problem is to explain the mechanisms that govern the reproduction of these classes of persons and the consequences of this social asymmetry on the interpersonal relationship between the individual buyer and the individual seller of labour power.

The relation between the single capitalist and the single worker is obviously linked to the relation between capitalists and workers as classes. But the necessary relation is the latter, not the former. None of the single interpersonal relations between individual capitalists and workers is really necessary to the reproduction of capitalism: each of them might terminate and capitalism would still go on. Only the general capital–labour relation is necessary for the working of capitalism. This is the sense in which class relations are *essential* for this mode of production.

This ontological argument suggests also a general method in the analysis of the single interpersonal relation between a capitalist and a worker. Each of these interpersonal relations has in fact its autonomy, but altogether they are socially constrained. This is why we cannot focus directly on a single relation in isolation but must start from the general class relation that conditions all of them.

Consider now how the neoclassical approach analyses the canonical interpersonal relation involving power: the relation between a boss and a worker in the workplace. By isolating this interpersonal relation from the social system, the eventual power relation of the former over the latter appears necessarily as a consequence of some particular feature of their interaction. The apparently innocent assumption of methodological individualism excludes that their interpersonal power relation might be caused by their different role in society – by the fact that one is a boss and the other a worker – and even makes the notion of exploitation between their social classes nonsensical.

This methodological choice however is not supported by any ontological argument. The asymmetry between the boss' and the worker's information sets and processing skills is simply supposed to exist, without any logical necessity. There is no attempt to explain how bosses might develop their superior talents and skills. Instead, neoclassical economics assumes that these interpersonal asymmetries already exist and, because of them, one individual becomes a boss and another a worker. If, for some reason, this inborn asymmetry changes or some imperfections in the decision making context evolve from one day to another, the theory implies that, immediately, the boss becomes a worker and vice versa. This is probably a nice abstract world, but it is not capitalism.

Ontologically, the boss and the worker are not merely individuals with inborn cognitive abilities adapting to an imperfect environment, but members of opposing classes. Their interaction does not occur in an abstract (perfect or imperfect) context in which individuals meet on the same ground but in the system of the bourgeoisie, a historical mode of production based on the exploitation of the working class by the capitalist class.

This is why, before introducing 'imperfections', it is necessary to fully develop the consequences of this social asymmetry. Without any need to imagine imperfect decision making contexts, interpersonal power can be explained as a manifestation of the social coercion imposed upon the working class: if, in the workplace, the boss commands and the worker obeys, it is not necessarily because one is better informed or more intelligent than the other, but because one is the agent of the exploiting class – and diligently accomplishes his role – and the other is a member of the exploited class, a person who brings 'his own hide to market and has nothing to expect but – a hiding' (Marx 1867, ch. 6). Knowledge and cognitive skills are probably correlated with the hierarchical position in the workplace but this is more the result of economic, social and cultural processes than the demonstration that the former are the cause of the latter. Even because the very specificity of capitalistic power is indeed that it is irrelevant who has better knowledge or cognitive skills: in any case, the agent of capital commands, and the worker obeys, even when the former is illiterate and the latter has a Ph.D.

From the outset, the choice of imperfections as explanatory categories of capitalist power relations is misleading. Imperfections might add useful elements to the explanation of the coercive forces of capitalism, but cannot be the cause of these forces for the simple reason that capitalism can work and develop even without them.

By contrast, without class relations, capitalist production could not even start. Nobody would choose an alienated job under exploitative conditions if he/she might opt for an economic rent without any duty to work. If neoclassical rational economic men really existed in this system, they would all choose to be capitalists, not workers, and the system would collapse before starting. Before adding new unnecessary explanatory categories of power and coercion, we must analyse the forms of power and coercion that emanate from this essential relation of capitalism. These forms of power and coercion are necessary in capitalism, exactly as the categories that explain them. An approach that discards social classes because of their incompatibility with methodological individualism has not many chances to get to the heart of capitalist power.

If we do not discuss the social nature of power in historically determined societies, with historically determined reproducing mechanisms, we cannot explain why in concrete situations, one individual has power over another. We may multiply *ad infinitum* the analysis of interpersonal power in isolation, under all possible sorts of imperfections, but, methodologically, these exercises cannot shed any light on the general coercion of capitalism and on its specificity with respect to other modes of production.

Historical materialism, exploitation and social coercion

From the perspective of historical materialism, the search of the universal causes of power in interpersonal relations is an empty question. Power relations are a consequence of the mode of organisation of society and change with the historical transformation of the latter. Societies are not universal and everlasting, but historically determined, and so are power relations. The scientific problem is not to isolate a particular interpersonal relation within an abstract society and verify its eventual power content according to a particular definition, but to explain the different forms of coercion that characterise the different historical modes of organisation of society.

Within the different aspects of the modes of organisation of society, historical materialism gives priority to the modes of production and exchange and to the corresponding modes of reproduction of the rules of social life. The laws of production and reproduction impose various forms of coercion on the members of society. Therefore, to explain the specific forms of power and coercion of capitalism, we must analyse the mechanisms of capitalist production and reproduction.

Marx and Engels have studied historically and theoretically how the development of the division of labour transforms the mode of production and the forms of social organisation. The transformation of the family, its internal organisation, its role in society and in the production process, the emergence of private property and social classes, the birth of the state and the rise of the capitalist mode of production are all parts of this historical process (Engels 1884). As they argue, these historical transformations do not follow a casual path but are governed and directed by particular economic forces and mechanisms. There is no need to push too far the role of these forces and mechanism, as mechanistic determinants of historical development, as some Marxists and Marx's critics have suggested. But we cannot either do as if they just did not exist and history were a completely random process.

A general feature of all class societies is exploitation. Exploitation might occur through different mechanisms: in the feudal system, for instance, it occurs through a direct power relation of the lord over the worker, which assures that a part of the crop produced by the latter goes to the former. In capitalism, as Marx has shown, this relation is mediated by the market and does not occur directly at an interpersonal level. This is why scientific critique is necessary to reveal the exploitative nature of capitalist production. Although apparently invisible, capitalist exploitation is in fact a logical consequence of capitalist class relations. Its existence is a consequence of this social relation between classes, independent from the relations between single individuals.

The existence of exploitation has direct implications in terms of power and coercion. Exploitation might not occur without some form of direct or indirect coercion. These forms of coercion may be analysed in different ways. But it is clear that a theory of capitalist power without social classes is a contradiction in terms. It equals to assume that social classes – the cause of exploitation of one part of society over another – have nothing to do with the mechanisms that force the members of one class to work for the members of the other class.

The forms of coercion that are necessary for the process of exploitation are different in different modes of production, but each class society needs its forms of social coercion in order to ensure that the exploited class produce not only for itself but also for the rest of society. Therefore, like exploitation, also social coercion is a necessary category in class societies. Its existence is not primarily a matter of empirical evidence, but one of logical necessity. In some modes of production, it may take the form of a set of empirically detectable interpersonal powers, but this is only a possibility, not a necessity. Logically, social coercion precedes the forms of power that may eventually appear at an interpersonal level.

A Marxist approach to power cannot thus accept the scientific question of neoclassical economics. The problem is not to explain how isolated individuals, with a natural propensity to exchange, decide to interact and, eventually, establish power relations between them. The problem is rather to discover the specific forms of social coercion of each class society and explain their relation with the prevailing mode of exploitation. In the case of capitalism, rather than seeking the universal features of power and their a-historical causes (such as imperfect information, uncertainty or bounded rationality), we must discover the forms of coercion that are necessary for the process of capitalist exploitation.

In defence of methodological individualism, one might imagine a sort of division of scientific labour, according to which methodological holists should be charged to study the existing forms of social coercion. Mathematically, if social coercion and individual power were linked by an additive relation, the results of these approaches might be added together. The limit of the individualist approach would then be simply in its partiality, not in its misleadingness: social coercion and interpersonal powers would exist side by side, but in no way one might influence or condition the other. Scientifically, methodological individualism and holism would be natural complements, each one shading light on one aspect of the problem.

Unfortunately, there exists no additive relation between social coercion and interpersonal power. We cannot add them because they are not independent. On the contrary, they are strictly interdependent and linked by a dialectical relation. Social coercion operates through, and is reproduced by, a multitude of interpersonal power relations. In turn, the existing forms of interpersonal power express the general coercion existing in society. This is my starting point in the study of social coercion and power relations within the framework of historical materialism.

Marx's critique of capital and the critique of power

The attempt to develop a dialectical relation between social coercion and interpersonal power raises a methodological problem: what is the correct – or simply the most convenient – order between the study of social coercion and interpersonal powers? Like Marx, I do not think that methodological choices can be taken for convenience. Rather, they must be defended ontologically. My idea, as I have anticipated, is to develop Marx's critique of capital, by discussing the forms of power and coercion emanating from capital accumulation.

Ontologically, Marx distinguishes clearly between what he calls 'total social capital' and the multitude of 'individual capitals' that forms it. As we will see in more details in the critique of competition, none of them is pure abstraction. They both exist in reality and the problem is to understand how they interact dialectically in the development of capitalism: how the development of total social capital imposes its logic on the development of its single constituents and how, in turn, the relations between individual capitals transforms concretely the dimension and the composition of total social capital.

The general methodological error of classical political economists, in Marx's view, is to cut this dialectical relation and deny any ontological and methodological role to the category of total social capital. In their conception, capital exists only as a set of independent individual capitals and the study of capital accumulation is reduced to an analysis of how individual capitals compete and interact with each other, under the implicit and incorrect assumption that the result of this interaction is socially unconstrained.

Against this conception, Marx starts with a systematic critique of total social capital before approaching the problem of competition between capitals. He first explains the laws of development of total social capital as necessary features of this mode of production and only then discusses how this systemic development imposes its laws on the relations between individual capitals. Marx takes two volumes of *Capital* to develop the analysis of total social capital before he can properly discuss competition between capitals, in volume three.

By remaining at the level of total social capital, social coercion already shows its essential role, as a necessary condition for the unfolding of the exploitative process. Its existence does not depend directly on asymmetric power relations between individuals but on the existence of total social capital.

A proper study of power, as a set of interpersonal relations, presupposes, however, a second step, a move to the level of the relations between individual capitals. Here, competition plays as a central role, not so much as the benchmark of power-free relations, as the neoclassical approach suggests, but as the enforcer of capital laws. If a world of perfect competition is really a world free from power relations or a world of social coercion depends on these laws of development of capital as a whole. The problem is that they are invisible at this ontological level and, without a critique of total social capital, it easily follows the assumption that they do not exist at all. This leads directly to a mystified conception in which competition appears as the best guarantee of freedom and equality.

With these premises, the logic of my critique can be presented schematically.

Marx's critique of capital can be decomposed in three logical moments: the critique of total social capital, the critique of competition and the synthesis of the two, namely, the critique of capitalism as a mystified system:

1 In the critique of total social capital – which logically precedes the critique of competition – Marx shows the exploitative nature of capitalist production.

2 His critique of competition shows how exploitation becomes invisible in the sphere of circulation, where individual capitals appear as autonomous and the relations between them appear as unconstrained and regulated simply by competition and equal exchange.

3 Taken together, these separated – but equally necessary – moments of Marx's critique show the mystified nature of capitalism as a system of exploitation hidden behind the veil of competition and equal exchange.

This articulated critique of capital has direct implications in terms of power and coercion:

1 Class exploitation presupposes the existence of forms of social coercion operating through social classes. These forms of coercion do not depend on competition and logically precede it.

2   Social coercion, however, is invisible in circulation, where interpersonal relations appear as independent from each other (and from the general relation of class exploitation) and regulated only by competition and individual freedom.

3   In their unity, these two moments of the critique show the mystified nature of capitalism as a system of social coercion hidden behind the veil of competition and individual freedom.

This logical scheme shows also the logical origin of the mystified conception developed by neoclassical theorists of power. The latter deny any logical separation between production and circulation and, like old vulgar economists, interpret all economic relations with the lenses of circulation. The logical steps behind this conception are the following:

1   Class exploitation and social coercion are not simply ignored but assumed to not exist.

2   As a consequence, competition is not seen as the mystified appearance, in the sphere of circulation, of the exploitative and coercing relations occurring in production, but as a faithful picture of equal exchange and individual freedom occurring in the economy in general. In this conception, power can exist only as a violation of the laws of competition.

3   The unity of these two moments provides a sophisticated rationalisation of the appearances of capitalism as a – or rather *the* – system of individual freedoms, in which power exists only as an eventual imperfection, caused by the lack of competition.

The rest of the book develops this logic, first as a critique of the neoclassical conception of power and then as an attempt to develop a Marxist conception of power and coercion in capitalism.

Structure of the book

I begin, in Chapter 2, by critically reviewing the debate on power in economics and by discussing the implicit ontology of power and competition as irreconcilable entities, operating in disjointed empirical realms. In Chapter 3, I argue that this conception is in fact part of a broader scientific program, often labelled as 'post Walrasian economics'. As such, it does not escape the internal problems of the post Walrasian research program. In Chapter 4, I move to external criticism and Marx. My goal is to demystify the illusion created by competition (and rationalised by neoclassical economics) that a world of perfect competition is an ideal power-free society. My critique is organised in three levels: methodology, ontology and ideology. In each of them, I develop Marx's critique of capital and I address it against the post Walrasian conception of power.

The second part of the book develops this critical path into an organic conception. In Chapter 5, I reconstruct Marx's analysis of competition and the role it plays in his general critique of capital and I criticise the neoclassical conception of perfect competition. Here, the critical and constructive elements for a Marxist theory of power and competition are reversed. The analysis builds explicitly on Marx's critique and the critique of the neoclassical conception comes as a corollary of Marx's general conception. In Chapter 6, I use Marx's critique of capital and competition to develop an ontology of power and coercion in capitalism. I show that in the capitalist ontology, competition plays a central role, as the coercive mechanism that regulates social and interpersonal relations. It is not at all the guarantor of power-free relations, but is rather a mechanism of social coercion finalised to economic exploitation.

The last chapter suggests how such a Marxist conception of power and competition in capitalism might reorient scientific research and the political struggle. The scientific and political problem is not only to understand capitalist power but also to invert the hegemonic tendency within bourgeois economics and political reformism to take the essential forms of capitalist coercion as natural and their development as unrestrainable.

Notes

1   The English translation can be misleading for the German term 'chance' (translated as 'probability') also means 'opportunity'.
2   The issue of power in political science is often associated to the work of Foucault. In his analysis, however, Foucault addresses various questions on different aspects of power, but, as he himself claims, he 'in no way construct[s] a theory of power' (Foucault 1990, p. 39). In his conception, power exists in a purely nominal sense rather than in any substantive sense: power 'is the name one attributes to a complex strategical relationship in a particular society' (Foucault 1980, p. 93). As Cousins and Hussain (1984) notice, Foucault's major interest is not in *what is power*, but in *how it is exercised*. As he says: 'Power is exercised rather than possessed' (Foucault 1977, p. 26); 'it only exists in action' (Gordon 1980 ed., p. 89). He also has no interest in quantification of power and disputes whether power comparability in any quantifiable form exists.
3   After Lukes' book, this reading of the debate in terms of 'dimensions' of power has become almost canonical in political and social theory. The term 'dimensions' of power, however, is misleading, since it suggests that power is a sort of vector, whose single elements are supposed to be independent from one another.
4   After the critique of Bachrach and Baratz, the one-dimensional view has been defended by Wolfinger (1971) and Polsby (1980).

5 This conception of power can be extended to Austrian economics as well. As Young (1995) shows, although Austrians consider the market as an arena of freedom in which interaction is purely voluntary, their conception of capitalism as essentially free from power relations presupposes atomism and competition. In Palermo (1998), I criticise the Austrian conception of the market process for its neglect of power relations in the explanation of the convergence of individual plans.

References

Arendt, Hannah (1970), *On violence*, London, The Penguin Press.

Bachrach, Peter and Morton Baratz (1962), Two faces of power, *American Political Science Review*, vol. 56, n. 4, pp. 947–52.

——(1963), Decisions and non decisions: An analytical framework, *The American Political Science Review*, vol. 57, pp. 632–42.

——(1970), *Power and poverty. Theory and practice*, New York, Oxford University Press.

Bottomore, Tom (1983 ed.), *A dictionary of Marxist thought*, Oxford, Blackwell Publishers Ltd.

Coase, Ronald (1937), The nature of the firm, *Economica*, vol. 4, n. 4, pp. 386–405.

Cousins, Mark and Athar Hussain (1984), *Michel Foucault*, Basingstoke, Macmillan.

Dahl, Robert (1961), *Who governs? Democracy and power in an American city*, New Haven and London, Yale University Press.

Engels, Frederick (1884), *The origin of the family, private property and the state*. Retrieved from www.marxists.org/archive/marx/works/1884/origin-family/index.htm (accessed 1 March 2016).

Foucault, Michel (1977), *Discipline and punish: The birth of the prison*, London, Allen Lane.

——(1980), *The history of sexuality, volume 1: An introduction*, London, Penguin.

——(1990), *Politics, philosophy, culture: Interviews and other writings 1977–1984*, New York, Routledge.

Gordon, Colin (1980 ed.), *Power/knowledge: Selected interviews and other writings by Michel Foucault 1972–1977*, New York, Pantheon.

Hunter, Floyd (1953), *Community power structure*, Chapel Hill, University of North Carolina Press.

Lukes, Steven (1974), *Power: A radical view*, London, Macmillan.

——(1982), Can the base be distinguished from the superstructure?, *Analyse & Kritik*, vol. 4, n. 2, pp. 211–22.

——(1983), Emancipation, in Bottomore, Tom (ed.), *A dictionary of Marxist thought*, Oxford, Blackwell Publishers Ltd.

——(1985), *Marxism and morality*, Oxford, Oxford University Press.

——(2005), *Power: A radical view – The original text with two major new chapters, 2nd edition*, Basingstoke, Palgrave Macmillan.

Marx, Karl (1867), *Capital: Critique of political economy, vol, 1, The process of capitalist production*. Retrieved from www.marxists.org/archive/marx/works/1867-c1/index.htm (accessed 1 March 2016).

Mills, Wright (1956), *The power elite*, New York, Oxford University Press.

Palermo, Giulio (1998), Economic power and the market process: A critique of the theory of convergence of Hayek and Kirzner, *Revista de Economia*, vol. 24, n. 22, pp. 49–77.

Parsons, Talcott (1957), The distribution of power in American society, *World Politics*, vol. 10, pp. 123–43.

——(1963A), On the concept of influence, *Public Opinion Quarterly*, vol. 27, pp. 37–62.

——(1963B). On the concept of political power, *Proceedings of the American Philosophical Society*, vol. 107, pp. 232–62.

Polsby, Nelson (1963), *Community power and political theory*, New Haven, Yale University Press.

——(1980), Potere locale e democrazia: Una critica empirica ai neo-elitisti, *Rivista Italiana di Scienza Politica*, vol. 10, n. 1, pp. 149–66.

Schattschneider, Elmer (1960), *The semi-sovereign people: A realist's view of democracy in America*, New York, Holt, Rinehart and Winston.

Weber, Max (1968), *Economy and society*, New York, Bedminster Press.

Williamson, Oliver (1975), *Markets and hierarchies: Analysis and antitrust implications: A study in the economics of internal organization*, New York, Free Press.

Wolfinger, Raymond (1971). Nondecisions and the study of local politics, *American Political Science Review*, vol. 65, pp. 1063–80.

Young, David (1995), The meaning and role of power in economic theories, in Groenewegen, John, Christos Pitelis and Sven-Erik Sjöstrand (eds), *On economic institutions: Theory and applications*, Aldershot, Edward Elgar.

Part I

Power in economics

2 The economic debate on power

It is common to see the firm characterized by the power to settle issues by fiat, by authority, or by disciplinary action superior to that available in the conventional market. This is delusion.

(Alchian and Demsetz 1972, p. 777)

The argument that the firm 'has no power of fiat, no authority, no disciplinary action any different in the slightest degree from ordinary market contracting' (Alchian and Demsetz, 1972, p.777) is exactly wrong: firms can and do exercise fiat that markets cannot.

(Williamson 1994, p. 325)

The exercise of power is ubiquitous in private exchange.

(Bowles and Gintis 2008, p. 1)

Although the notions of power, coercion and domination have been discussed since the beginning of political economy by authors such as Adam Smith, Marx and Friedrich Wieser, the modern academic debate rarely goes back to these authors. Rather, the role of power in economics has come to the forefront of the academic debate in the seventies, mainly as a byproduct of the debate on the nature of the firm, with contrasting contributions from Alchian and Demsetz (1972) on the one hand and Stephen Marglin (1974, 1975) on the other. The former contend that formal authority within the firm is only an appearance, which hides however a reality of perfect reciprocal freedom between the boss and the worker; the latter argues instead that power relations play a decisive role in the organisation of the firm. However, Coase's (1937) paper on the nature of the firm is in the background. In this paper, Coase explicitly sets the mechanisms of authority and command within the firm against the market price mechanism as alternative modes of coordination.

Recall that Coase's paper is not about the nature of capitalist power relations; rather, it addresses 'the nature of the firm' in capitalism. From a Marxist perspective, such a problem may appear trivial because the firm is an integral part of the capitalist system. Therefore, Marxists suggest that by analysing the historical origin and developments of capitalism one can understand the nature of the firm and of the other institutions of capitalism.

This problem, however, is anything but trivial if it is placed within the context of neoclassical economics, a context in which economic institutions are seen as universal and everlasting, like the economic problem they solve: the allocation of scarce resources. In neoclassical economics, the firm and the market are two alternative allocative mechanisms. The theoretical problem is that in the general equilibrium model, coordination between isolated individuals, both in the sphere of production and in that of consumption, occurs entirely within the market, which makes all other institutions economically redundant. The story told to describe the general equilibrium model sometimes refers to the firm and to other institutions (such as the family), but analytically, they are superfluous add-ons. This leaves the internal relations of the firm undetermined. As Paul Samuelson (1957, p. 894) put it, 'In a perfectly competitive model, it really doesn't matter who hires whom; so let labor hire capital'.

The general equilibrium model, like any theoretical model with decision makers, is defined by a 'decision making context' (DMC) and an 'organisational structure' (OS). The former defines the features of the world in which agents interact and the decision making criteria they use: it specifies the eventual existence of risk or uncertainty, of logical or historical time, the information sets of the agents, their perfect or imperfect knowledge of these sets and their kind of full or bounded rationality. The latter defines the type of relations among agents and the way in which the latter interact: it describes the effects of the action of one agent over the others, the eventual presence of hierarchical or power relations and, in the case of market interaction, the market forms prevailing in the different sectors of the economy.

The DMC of the Walrasian model is characterised by perfect information, full rationality, and zero transaction costs. I will refer to it as the 'perfect' DMC. The OS is completely decentralised, based on market relations and perfect competition.

Starting from the fact that the firm is redundant within the Walrasian model, Coase raises two scientific questions: Why do hierarchies exist in the market system? What is the source of power relations within the firm? To answer these questions, Coase explores the reasons why authority and direction may be economically superior to market relations in a context of positive transaction costs. Methodologically, Coase rejects the perfect DMC and investigates how OSs with some degree of centralisation might perform better than the Walrasian one. Within this logic, Coase's explanation of the nature of the firm insists on the existence within the firm of a relation of formal authority that is absent in the market. Thus, in one way or another, Coase introduces a form of power in the neoclassical model and uses it to analytically characterise the firm as an institution that is qualitatively distinct from the market. If power is the ability to condition the behaviours of other individuals, then intra-firm authority is a very strong form of power because it implies that one subject orders and the other obeys.

Theoretically, the introduction of authority as a specific coordination mechanism operating within the firm solves Coase's problem (the nature of the firm). However, it disrupts the harmonious vision of interpersonal relations provided by the Walrasian model. From the viewpoint of the liberal doctrine, the problem is thus to reconstruct a harmonious vision of spontaneous (and possibly Pareto-efficient) interactions in a context in which, alongside the competitive mechanism of the market, there exists a mechanism of command working within the firm.

Some forty years after its publication, Coase's paper has become the starting point for a new research program aiming to explain all the institutions of capitalism and their internal power relations. This research program has been developed, in particular, by the new institutional economics, whose growing impact in the economic debate led to reward Coase, in 1991, with the Nobel prize. In my interpretation of this school of thought, research has developed along two distinct lines. In the former, Coase's intuition has been developed by denying the existence of real authority relations within the firm and by explaining the mechanism of command as a specific form of competition. The main exponents of this line of research are Alchian and Demsetz. In the second approach, the costs and benefits of competition and command have been analysed systematically in an attempt to determine the virtues and vices of markets and hierarchies. Williamson's transaction costs economics and the property rights theory of Hart and Moore are the main contributors to this line.[1] Outside of new institutional economics, this research on power and the institutions of capitalism has been developed, in particular, by exponents of radical political economics, such as Bowles and Gintis, and of the institutional school, such as Goldberg.

Although all these approaches have confronted each other in harsh polemical tones, my thesis is that the common acceptance of neoclassical methodology (and its implicit ontology) has allowed rich exchanges between them and has produced a convergence towards a common conception of power, as an exception to Walrasian competition. By contrast, Marxist contributions, based on a different method, have remained mainly at the margins of the debate and, when discussed explicitly, have often been misinterpreted and read with neoclassical lenses. This problem does not involve only historians of economic thought. Rather, I argue that the neoclassical method engenders a narrow conception of power as a purely interpersonal relation, which incorporates all the contradictions noted by Marx against the bourgeois political economy and which hides, rather than revealing, the specific forms of social coercion of the capitalist mode of production.

I begin by reviewing the main theoretical approaches developed in the debate. Then, I single out the common methodological and ontological traits of these approaches, and I propose a representation in terms of set theory of their different positions concerning the extension of power relations in capitalism.

The contractual approach of Alchian and Demsetz

The idea that capitalism is characterised by the absence of any substantial power relations among individuals has been vigorously defended by Alchian and Demsetz within their 'contractual approach' (Alchian and Demsetz 1972, Jensen and Meckling 1976, Cheung 1983, 1987, 1992). Their 1972 paper is one of the most frequently cited contributions to interpersonal relations within the firm and has become the starting point for a new theoretical approach. In their 'property rights approach', they explicitly deny the existence of any form of power or authority even in contexts in which, according to many, these forms are clearly manifest.

The authors consider production within the firm as the result of the cooperation of individuals belonging to a team. The essential feature of team production is the impossibility of determining the relative contribution of each component of the team to the final production, which makes it difficult 1) to fix the efficient remuneration of the different work activities and 2) to prevent negligent and free-riding behaviours within the team. Such difficulties raise a problem of monitoring. Based on the assumption that the benefits of monitoring (the increase of overall productivity) are greater than its costs (the wage of the monitor), it follows that there is an incentive to establish a monitor. The monitor, however, has no real power over the other members of the team because he is subject to the same discipline imposed by market competition: he would be replaced as soon as another member of the team offered the same monitoring activity at a lower price. In this way, Alchian and Demsetz bring all the relations within the firm back to market relations and show that hierarchy within the firm is only apparent. This is how they discuss the employer–worker relationship.

> It is common to see the firm characterized by the power to settle issues by fiat, by authority, or by disciplinary action superior to that available in the conventional market. This is delusion. The firm does not own all

its inputs. It has no power of fiat, no authority, no disciplinary action any different in the slightest degree from ordinary market contracting between any two people. I can 'punish' you only by withholding future business or by seeking redress in the courts for any failure to honor our exchange agreement. That is exactly all that any employer can do. He can fire or sue, just as I can fire my grocer by stopping purchases from him or sue him for delivering faulty products.

(Alchian and Demsetz 1972, p. 777)

According to Alchian and Demsetz, the reason why power relations should have no place in theory is that they do not exist in reality. Additionally, the opposition between firms and markets is only illusory. The market is universal, and perfect competition is always at work, even within the firm. The firm is nothing but a particular form of the market – one in which price is not continually re-negotiated, although the outcome is as if it were.

This position has been abundantly criticised by Marxist historians and radical economists who, in contrast, see the organisation of the firm as strictly dependent on the question of power (Braverman 1974, Marglin 1974, 1975, 1991, Edwards 1979). But perhaps the best way to appreciate the limits of this approach is by following its internal development and its inevitable dead end.

To deny the existence of power relations within the firm, Alchian's pupil, Stephen Cheung, finds nothing better than denying the existence of the firm itself as an object of the social realm. In his view, what we generally call a 'firm' is, in fact, simply a complex nexus of market contracts. The firm itself is a sort of market and is thus theoretically indistinguishable from it. Hence, the concept of the *firm* is unimportant and theoretically useless. No one is clearer than the author himself:

It is often the case that the entrepreneur who holds employment contracts (and it is not clear whether it is the entrepreneur who employs the worker or the worker who employs the entrepreneur) may contract with other firms; a contractor may sub-contract; a sub-contractor may sub-sub-contract further; and a worker may contract with a number of 'employers' or 'firms'. ... With this approach the size of the firm becomes indeterminate and unimportant.

(Cheung 1987, p. 57)

If we cannot in any meaningful economic sense identify 'firms', as separate entities, we do not know what a firm is when we see one in the real world.

(Cheung 1992, p. 56)[2]

Cheung's contribution is peculiar: he assumes that markets are universal and everlasting and, on this basis, carries Alchian and Demsetz's approach to its logical conclusion. Faced with the inevitable conflict between his theory and reality, he does not reconsider critically his theory, but rejects, on theoretical grounds, the existence of the reality he wished to explain. In his theory of the firm, firms do not exist!

Williamson's transaction costs economics

Williamson's contributions constitute the most systematic attempt to develop Coase's intuitions and approach the problem of institutions within transaction costs economics (Coase 1937, Williamson 1975, 1985, 1994, 1995, 1996A, 1996B, 2003, 2005, Williamson and Ouchi 1983, Simon 1951, 1991). For these contributions, in 2009, Williamson won the Nobel prize. His market-hierarchies framework is explicitly defined within an individualist methodology and is developed by means of neoclassical analytical tools. However, Williamson explicitly distances himself from the approach of Alchian and Demsetz:

> The argument that the firm 'has no power of fiat, no authority, no disciplinary action any different in the slightest degree from ordinary market contracting' (Alchian and Demsetz, 1972, p.777) is exactly wrong: firms can and do exercise fiat that markets cannot.
>
> (Williamson 1994, p. 325)

In Williamson's theory, firms are explained by determining the conditions that make a centralised OS more efficient than the market in a context of positive transaction costs.[3] His method can be described as follows. He assumes, 'for expositional convenience, that "in the beginning there were markets"' (1975, p. 21) and, through successive exercises in comparative statics, introduces non-market institutions – based on different forms of hierarchy and authority – every time the market fails to allocate resources efficiently. Finally, by interpreting these comparative statics exercises as if they described a real historical process, Williamson provides his explanation of the existing institutional configuration of modern capitalist economies.

In this approach, markets and hierarchies are considered alternative instruments to the same end (to complete transactions), and their existence is explained in terms of their relative efficiency. If markets and hierarchies coexist in reality, it is because transaction costs prevent either of them from solving the entire allocation problem efficiently. Their relation is thus one of substitution. Once hierarchy is introduced, the (virtual) process of substitution proceeds until the economic benefits of centralisation exceed the economic costs. In this way, Williamson explains not only the nature of the firm but also its boundaries because the optimal degree of centralisation defines the optimal dimension of the firm.

Williamson's 'market and hierarchies' framework is built on three theoretical categories: 1) opportunism, 2) bounded rationality, and 3) asset specificity. The simultaneous presence of 1), 2), and 3) produces transaction costs and prevents any single institution from allocating resources efficiently.[4] The advantages of hierarchy over the market stem from the fact that hierarchy 1) reduces opportunism (both by means of authority and by stimulating solidarity), 2) attenuates problems stemming from bounded rationality (by facilitating adaptive sequential decision making processes in situations in which contracts on the contingent states of nature are not possible and spot markets are risky), and 3) lowers bargaining costs caused by asset specificity (both through authority and by generating convergent expectations between the parties). The benefits of markets with respect to hierarchy include 1) the incentive mechanism of competition and 2) the growing diseconomies associated with hierarchical organisation.

The assumption of bounded rationality as an initial category of Williamson's framework is problematic and, as we will see, is abandoned in the development of the new property rights school. In fact, this assumption conflicts with the fundamental assumption of Williamson's method, namely that institutional evolution follows economic efficiency. Put simply, on the one hand, individuals are supposed to be rationally bounded; on the other hand, their *sub-optimal* decisions are supposed to select *optimal* institutional configurations (cf. Granovetter 1985, Hodgson 1988, 1991, 1993A, 1993B, 1994).

The first application of the market and hierarchies framework concerns the work relation. As Christos Pitelis (1991, p. 13) notes, this application is particularly important because only the work relation can explain the emergence of hierarchies from a situation of pure markets. All other applications of Williamson's framework (vertical integration, M-form, conglomerates) presuppose the existence of the firm and thus address the problem of the *evolution* of the firm, not its *origins*. The (hierarchical) work relation represents, in the story that starts with 'in the beginning there were markets', the first suppression of the market. All other changes in the internal structure of the firm and in the relations among firms are *subsequent* and presuppose a certain degree of hierarchy (i.e., the existence of a work relation). If at *time 0* there were only markets, at *time 1* there are markets and hierarchical work relations (i.e., firms). Then, from *time 2* onward, the more complex forms of power relations can develop.

The importance of the work relation in the explanation of the firm makes Williamson's framework unlike Alchian and Demsetz's approach. Williamson's framework implies 1) a clear-cut distinction between the firm and the market based on the presence/absence of hierarchical relations and 2) a distinction between the work relation and other economic relations (such as the grocer–customer relation).

The property rights approach of Hart and Moore

The new theory of property rights (or simply 'the theory of property rights') developed by Hart and Moore finds its inspiration in the original contribution of Alchian and Demsetz (1972). At the same time, it aims to overcome the lack of formal analysis of transaction costs economics, whose arguments have been developed mainly verbally (Grossman and Hart 1983, 1986, Hart 1988, 1989, 1990, 1995, 1996, Hart and Moore 1988, 1990, 2005, 2007, 2008, Moore 1992). As far as the issue of power is concerned, this theory is closer to the approach of Williamson (so much so that it is often presented as a sophisticated version of it) and reaches, in many ways, quite opposite conclusions with respect to the original property rights theory of Alchian and Demsetz.

Like transaction costs economics, the property rights school assumes an imperfect DMC in which contracts are necessarily incomplete. However, contract incompleteness depends solely on imperfect information, as in Alchian and Demsetz's approach, unlike Williamson's theory, in which it also depends on bounded rationality. According to Hart (1990), the problem is not that agents are not capable of conceiving of all possible contingencies but rather that it is impossible, or extremely costly, for a third party (a tribunal) to verify the execution of the contract. In other words, individuals are not bounded in their cognitive abilities but in their ability to communicate to a third party the terms of their agreement. Bounded rationality is thus unimportant for a theory of institutions. Therefore, this approach overcomes the contradiction between rationally bounded individuals and efficient institutional arrangements that characterises Williamson's framework.

Hart and Moore analyse the problem of when transactions should be conducted within a firm or through the market. They classify contractual rights into two categories: specific and residual rights. The former are the rights explicitly specified in the contract; the latter are the rights to use assets according to one's wishes in all cases not mentioned in the contract. Residual rights are conferred by ownership. The owner of an asset can decide how it should be used and by whom (of course, within the constraints imposed by law and specific contracts). In particular, he is entitled to prevent the other party from using his assets in case of disputes. When, for party A, the cost of listing all specific rights over an asset of party B is high, it might be optimal for party A to purchase all residual rights. In this way, by assuming ownership of the specific asset, A acquires the residual rights of control over it and can dispose of it as he wishes.

With this classification, the authors provide a straightforward definition of the firm and its boundaries with the market. A firm is identified with the physical assets its owners control. If two assets have the same owner, then they form a single, integrated firm; if they have different owners, then they form two separate firms, and the relation between them is a market one. Decisions about integration or non-integration are important because control over assets gives the owner decision making power in the event of unforeseen contingencies. This situation has consequences both on the grounds of efficiency and on the grounds of power relations.

From the viewpoint of efficiency, this approach studies how changes in ownership affect the incentives of both workers and owner-managers. With respect to the famous Coase (1960) theorem, contract incompleteness implies that the distribution of property rights has efficiency consequences. In contrast to transaction costs economics, Hart and Moore argue that the relevant comparison is not between the non-integrated outcome and the complete contract outcome; this would assume that integration yields the outcome that would arise under complete contracts. In a context of imperfect information and asset specificity, however, integration does not remove the incentives for opportunistic behaviour; it simply modifies them depending on which party purchases residual rights. In any case, opportunism creates distortions that prevent the theoretical first-best solution – defined under complete contracts – from being obtained. Therefore, the relevant comparison is between three necessarily inefficient situations: non-integration and integration with either A or B acquiring residual rights.

Ownership of physical assets, however, is a matter not only of efficiency but also of power. According to this approach, the power of the boss over the worker is a consequence of his ownership of physical assets within a context of imperfect information. As Moore (1992, p. 496–7) puts it, 'A boss exerts authority over workers because, in the event of a dispute, he can deny access to important physical assets'. This solves the paradox of Alchian and Demsetz's grocer, based on the assumption that the work relation is not qualitatively different from any other market relation:

> When a customer 'fires' Alchian and Demsetz's grocer, the grocer (being a separate contractor) gets to keep the store; whereas if the grocer were an employee of the customer, the customer (the boss) could deny the grocer (the worker) access to the store, and could hire another grocer on the spot labor market.
>
> (Moore 1992, p. 497)

Methodologically, there are no significant differences between the approach of Hart and Moore and the contractualist one. However, their theoretical treatment of imperfections leads to opposite conclusions, to the point that Hart (1995, p. 5) suggests, 'Given its concern with power, the approach proposed ... has something in common with Marxian theories of the capitalist–worker relationship'. We will see, however, that this similarity is only formal and that the different method followed by Marx, which is not based on 'imperfections', leads to a completely different conception of power relations in capitalism.

The radical political economics of Bowles and Gintis

Bowles and Gintis' contested exchange framework is the most developed attempt to analyse power within radical political economics (Bowles 1985, Bowles and Gintis 1988, 1990, 1993A, 1993B, 1993C, 1993D 1994A, 1994B, 2000, 2012, Gintis 1989, Gintis, and Ishikawa 1981, Bowles, Gintis and Gustafsson 1993 eds, Bowles, Franzini and Pagano 2004 eds, Putterman 1982, 1984, 1993, 1995, Screpanti 2001).[5] Its goal is to show that power relations are not confined within the boundaries of the firm, but exist in competitive markets as well.

The authors define competition as a situation characterised by free entry and large numbers of buyers and sellers, but not by market clearing. With this definition, they demonstrate that even in competitive equilibrium (with non-clearing markets), a market economy sustains a system of power relations among agents (a competitive equilibrium is a situation in which actors are incapable of improving their position by altering variables over which they have control).[6] This result is obtained by relaxing one of the assumptions of the Walrasian DMC that Bowles and Gintis (like Hart and Moore) consider the most implausible: the assumption that contract enforcement by a third party is costless and unproblematic.

Bowles and Gintis (1993A, p. 325) define power as 'the capacity of some agents to influence the behavior of others to their advantage through the threat of imposing sanctions'. The absence of power relations in the Walrasian model is a consequence of the condition that supply equals demand, which implies that each agent loses nothing by abandoning his optimal transaction in favour of his next best alternative: in equilibrium, the cost to agent B of foregoing an exchange with agent A is zero, so that A cannot affect B's wellbeing by terminating the relation. Hence, Bowles and Gintis continue, A has no power over B. More generally, the fact that in Walrasian equilibria no agent can impose sanctions on other agents implies that the economy works without any underlying power relation among agents.

If contract enforcement is problematic, however, the picture changes radically. Bowles and Gintis (1993A, p. 332) 'call an exchange *contested*, when B's good or service possesses an attribute that is valuable to A, is costly for *B* to provide, yet is not fully specified in an enforceable contract'. When exogenous contract enforcement cannot be guaranteed at zero cost by a third party (such as the judicial system), the transacting parties must enforce their agreement by themselves. In this case, the terms of the transaction are determined by the monitoring and sanctioning mechanisms instituted by *A* to induce *B* to provide the desired level of the contested attribute. One such enforcement mechanism is *contingent renewal*: 'contingent renewal obtains when *A* elicits performance from *B* by promising to renew the contract in future periods if satisfied, and to terminate the contract if not' (1993A, p. 333).

A typical example of contested exchange is the employer–worker relationship, in which 'while the employer's promise to pay the wage is legally enforceable, the worker's promise to bestow an adequate level of effort … is not' (Bowles and Gintis 1993A, p. 333). Other examples studied by Bowles and Gintis are the relationships between owner and manager, lender and borrower, and between parties in international exchanges (Gintis 1989, Bowles, Gintis and Gustafsson 1993 eds, Bowles and Gintis 1994B). In all these cases, competitive equilibrium is characterised by non-clearing markets, and agents on the *short side* of the market have power over the agents on the *long side* with whom they transact (where excess supply exists, the demand side is the short one, and vice versa).

The cause of this power relation is that the agents on the long side who are lucky enough to enter the relation with agents on the short side enjoy the 'enforcement rent' (in the case of the employer–worker relationship, the 'employment rent'), defined as the difference between the utility they obtain thanks to the transaction and the utility they would have if the transaction terminates. The fact that within imperfect DMCs perfectly competitive markets do not necessarily clear produces thus an asymmetry between the two sides of the market, which, in turn, affects interpersonal relations between single buyers and sellers.

The employment rent is the instrument by which the employer places the worker under constant threat and compensate him/her for the nuisance of being commanded (similarly, Bowles and Gintis show that creditors have power over debtors and owners of enterprises have power over managers). It is thus the fact that unemployment is harder than work that confers a power of retaliation to the employer over the worker and that makes the latter provide an 'adequate' level of effort at work.

Bowles and Gintis' theory indirectly sheds light on the theoretical consistency of Alchian and Demsetz's claim that intra-firm relations are power-free. In fact, within non-clearing markets, contrary to what Alchian and Demsetz assume, free-contracting engenders power relations between the parties. The problem of Alchian and Demsetz's approach can thus be seen as follows: to say that the firm is a form of (competitive) market is not sufficient to prove that intra-firm relations are power-free simply because, as Bowles and Gintis demonstrate, perfectly competitive markets within an imperfect DMC can still involve power. If Alchian and Demsetz had remained coherent with their imperfect DMC, they would have realised that, in an imperfect grocer's market, they could no longer fire their grocer at zero cost. The idea that the worker can leave the capitalist without utility losses, holds true only within the perfect DMC. Outside of it, it is generally costly to leave an interpersonal relation and individuals may be willing to accept some form of power, even if just for personal convenience.

With respect to new institutionalism, Bowles and Gintis provide a completely different picture of capitalism. They show that (non-Walrasian) competitive equilibria are generally characterised by involuntary unemployment and by wage differentials based on gender or race (or on other characteristics that have nothing to do with productivity), that the democratic firm is superior to the capitalist one, and that capitalism is technologically inefficient. Most importantly, the result that power relations exist even under voluntary market exchange collapses the picture of a harmonious society that is provided by standard Walrasian economics and reconstructed by new institutional economics. Outside the Walrasian world, when markets do not necessarily clear, the market can no longer be seen as an arena of free interactions devoid of coercion, as liberal political philosophy suggests.

Notwithstanding these theoretical differences, Bowles and Gintis' approach is not methodologically different from those developed by new institutionalists and ultra-liberals: imperfections are the cause of power relations, and a battery of models formalising all different sorts of imperfections existing in the real world is the way to shed light on capitalistic power relations.

Methodologically and theoretically, there is also a large convergence between Bowles and Gintis' approach and the 'efficiency wages' literature, focusing on workers' 'shirking' in the presence of imperfect information and incomplete contracts (Shapiro and Stiglitz 1984, Akerlof and Yellen 1986 eds, Greenwald and Stiglitz 1988, 1993). In both cases, a wage higher than the market clearing one induces the worker to work harder than he/she wishes. The main difference is that, in the radical approach, imperfections are explanatory causes of power relations and, in this branch of new Keynesian economics, they are the cause of allocation inefficiencies and second best solutions (rigorously speaking, efficiency wages have to do with productivity, not with efficiency, because total output is not increased by taking inputs constant, but by increasing one of them, namely labour). However, these approaches share the idea that imperfections are the necessary ingredients to understand power and inefficiency. In the words of Bruce Greenwald and Joseph Stiglitz (1993, p. 24), 'Modern Keynesians have identified these real world "imperfections" as the source of the problem: leaving them out of the model is like leaving Hamlet out of the play'.[7]

Goldberg's institutional perspective

Things are no different with Goldberg's (1976, 1980) theory, which aims to build a bridge between new institutional economics and radical economics (the author takes Williamson and Richard Edwards as spokespersons of these economic schools). Although he is close to the old American institutional tradition, Goldberg develops this exercise by following methodological individualism. First, however, let us consider Edwards' (1979) position.

By explicitly referring to Marx (1867), Edwards reconsiders the distinction between labour and labour power: *labour power*, which is the commodity that the employer buys, is the capacity to perform certain types of productive activity; *labour* is the active, concrete process performed by the worker. Actual labour activity is determined not only by labour power but also by the ability of the employer to extract labour from labour power. In Edwards, as well as in Marx, this distinction is used to explain exploitation (exploitation is seen here as a manifestation of economic power).

The process of the extraction of labour from labour power has been the object of a wide research program within the Marxist-radical tradition. Edwards, in particular, notes that in this concrete process, there may be a discrepancy between what the employer buys in the market and what he needs for production. In Goldberg's reading of Edwards, this discrepancy is due to imperfections in the DMC. He thus assumes a DMC of imperfect information, opportunistic individuals, costly contract enforcement, and historical time. In such an imperfect DMC, the extraction of labour from labour power is problematic because imperfections prevent the parties from precisely knowing, at the time of contracting, the labour that will be extracted in the labour process.

According to the author, this situation gives rise to discrepancies between *promise* and *execution*, making room for the exercise of power. In other words, Goldberg does not interpret Edwards' claim that the labour contract is exploitative as a consequence of the class structure of the economy, as Edward himself suggests, but as a consequence of some empirical specificity of the work relation, such as the fact that working takes time and that information in the workplace is not perfect. The empirical attributes of the work relation are so interpreted as *causes* of power in capitalism.

However, Goldberg continues, a discrepancy between promise and execution may arise every time a relation between two parties is not instantaneous, as in the Walrasian world. Therefore, it is not peculiar to the employment relation, as Marxists contend, but characterises, to varying degrees, most exchange relations (Goldberg 1980, pp. 252–3). Goldberg concludes that power relations are not confined within the firm because an incentive not to keep a promise may emerge in several types of contractual relations, even outside the firm.

Also in this case, power relations exist only if contracting is problematic, and problematic contracting is a consequence of imperfections in the DMC. Rather than a bridge between new institutionalism and Marxism, Goldberg's theory is a neoclassical interpretation of Marx, which leads to a conception of power that, in many respects, is the opposite of the Marxian one. Theories of value and exploitation are not seen as essential aspects of Marx's work of demystification of the capitalist mode of production but as useless social notions without implications in terms of interpersonal power relations. As I will argue, however, for Marx, capitalist exploitation has nothing to do with a discrepancy between *promise* and *execution*. On the contrary, Marx shows that capitalists promise to exploit workers, and the point is that they generally keep this promise.

The terms of the debate

All the approaches discussed above share the idea that power relations exist only within imperfect DMCs. Authors who explicitly adhere to the liberal doctrine believe that the perfect DMC is the rule in reality. In their view, this justifies the fact that economic theory ignores power relations, at least in its general formulation. By contrast, their rivals in the debate on power consider the Walrasian DMC unrealistic. With asymmetric information, uncertainty, historical time, bounded rationality, or other imperfections, they argue, interpersonal relations necessarily involve power.

Ontologically, these apparently competing theories develop the same conception of reality, according to which the existence of power depends on the features of the DMC in which agents interact. In a perfect DMC, there is no room for power relations: the internal structure of the firm is irrelevant, and competition clears all markets; therefore, no one can have power over anyone else. In imperfect DMCs, by contrast, intra-firm relations affect the firm's performance, and markets do not necessarily clear. In these circumstances, they argue, power relations can emerge both within the firm and within the market. Therefore, in all these theories, imperfections are the *cause* of power relations. Eliminate them, these authors maintain – either implicitly or explicitly – and power relations disappear.

The problem of power is thus an empirical one, and its solution is to be found in the relevance of imperfections in the real world. According to this ontology, economic reality is split into two distinct closed systems: a system with no imperfection, in which interpersonal relations are governed by perfect competition, and a system with imperfections, in which power matters.

Although this ontology remains mostly implicit in the discourse of neoclassical economists, it is the sole justification of their methodology, according to which economic reality must be explained by two (incompatible but complementary) sets of models: a model of Walrasian competition, explaining the relations within the perfect DMC, and a set of models of economic power, explaining interpersonal relations within the parts of the system characterised by imperfect DMCs (it goes without saying that the former defines the body of economic theory, whereas the latter serves to explain what the former cannot).

At first sight, authors who consider imperfections pervasive in the real world do not need this ontological assumption. Within the radical school, Ernesto Screpanti (2001, p. 145) is explicit on this point. He begins by defining a complex DMC characterised by bounded rationality, imperfect information, uncertainty, and various externalities and then affirms, 'Perfect and atomistic competition cannot exist in this world, even as a limit case – I mean the neoclassical competition that eliminates all inefficiencies and power hubris'. In his view, the perfect DMC is only a theoretical benchmark with no empirical counterpart. It is not an ontological entity of capitalist economies but a methodological tool of the economist. The model of perfect competition does not serve to understand how the real world works but how it does not. To describe real capitalist economies, instead, one must assume an imperfect DMC. With this interpretation, however, it is not clear why Screpanti and other neoclassical radicals choose this abstract fiction with no ontological role as the theoretical benchmark of their supposedly more realistic exercises.

This underlying ontology explains why theoretical investigations of power relations started from the firm, a domain in which hierarchy and authority are so evident as to be considered *the phenomena to explain*. In a first stage of the debate, the fact that market relations have been depicted as power-free has led to an analysis of power (within the firm) as an exception to the general model (of the market). This situation has led to the question of 'the boundaries of the firm', as if the firm, with its authority relations, were antagonistic to the market, with its power-free relations. In this way, the complementary role of the firm and the market in capitalism is necessarily lost.

The successive step in the debate, consisting of questioning the assumption that power is effectively confined within the firm, led finally to a more accurate redefinition of the problem. The theoretical question became the following: where are the boundaries of economic power? Or, to put it in the antagonist terms of this approach, where is the demarcation line between power and power-free relations?

With this narrow definition of the problem, the sphere of existence of power relations and that of power-free relations can be represented in terms of set theory. The set of existing economic relations can be divided into two disjoint subsets according to the absence/presence of imperfections in the DMC. The borderline between these subsets separates the parts of the world in which interpersonal relations are governed by Walrasian competition from those in which they are governed by power. This ontology can be represented graphically with the convention that the perfect DMC is on the left of the borderline and imperfect DMCs are on the right.

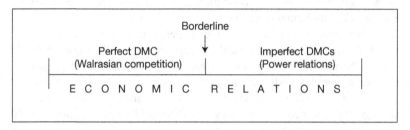

Figure 2.1 The boundaries of economic power

If we allow the borderline to move from left to right, the sphere of existence of power relations is progressively compressed. As limit cases, if the borderline is at the left boundary of economic relations, we have a conception according to which power relations embrace the entire economy. If it is at the right boundary, we have a conception of the economy as involving no power relations, formally represented by the general equilibrium model.

In this representational scheme, the approach of Alchian and Demsetz is the most radical one on the right-hand side. They see perfect competition everywhere, even when this mode of interaction is actually suppressed by other economic mechanisms.

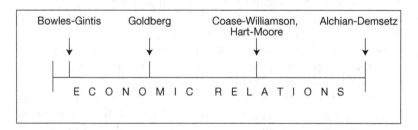

Figure 2.2 The terms of the debate

For this reason, they deny the existence of any power relation in the economy and compress the sphere of existence of power into the empty set. Their underlying DMC, however, is ambiguous. On the one hand, to explain the firm, Alchian and Demsetz explicitly introduce imperfect information in the DMC; on the other hand, they implicitly assume a perfect DMC when they claim that the employer has no real power over his workers. Faced with this contradiction, the authors remain caught in the middle. However, Cheung takes a well-defined route: to coherently defend the thesis that there is no power in capitalism, he returns to the perfect DMC, a context in which power relations disappear but the firm disappears as well, exactly as in the general equilibrium model.

In contrast to this position, new institutional economists, such as Coase and Williamson, or Hart and Moore, recognise that power relations do exist. They explicitly define imperfect DMCs to explain the firm and identify power relations with intra-firm relations. For this reason, they restrict the analysis of power relations to the particular forms that these relations acquire within the firm, namely, authority and hierarchy. At the same time, they concede that outside the firm, in the market, there is no room for power. Like Alchian, Demsetz, and Cheung, they assume that the boundaries of power coincide with those of the firm. Unlike these authors, however, Coase, Williamson, Hart and Moore do not see the firm as an implicit (perfectly competitive) market but rather as an alternative (and, under certain conditions, more efficient) allocative mechanism.

Bowles and Gintis, on the one hand, and Goldberg, on the other, make a further step to the left and show that power relations exist even beyond the boundaries of the firm, to the extent that markets are imperfect. It is not clear whether Bowles and Gintis push the borderline between power and Walrasian competition to the far left boundary of economic relations. The authors explicitly contend that power relations are ubiquitous in real capitalist economies, which might suggest that there is no room for power-free relations in their conception. However, this is only because they see imperfections as pervasive in the real world. Just as for their less radical colleagues, the sphere of existence of power relations coincides with the diffusion of imperfections in the DMC. Therefore, if it happens in a particular market that demand equals supply, then their theory implies that within such a subset of the economic realm, interpersonal relations are power-free. Therefore, neoclassical radicals do not challenge the orthodox conception of power relations. Their radicalism consists simply of moving the borderline a bit more to the left. At the same time, however, it is entirely internal to the logic of mainstream economics, a logic according to which imperfections are the *cause* of power relations.

Notes

1 In Palermo (2000), I argue that in both these streams of new institutionalism there is a tension between two conflicting goals: first, to characterise theoretically the capitalist firm and, second, to show the power-free nature of capitalism. In Ankarloo and Palermo (2004), we focus the critique on Williamson's transaction costs economics.

2 Becker's (1992, p. 68) comment is sharp: 'We generally know a firm when we see one'.

3 Transaction costs are never defined in Williamson's work. Quoting the (not very precise) definition of Arrow (1969, p. 48), Williamson (1985, p. 18) refers to the 'costs of running the system'; later on (Williamson, 1985, p. 19), he defines them as 'the equivalent of friction in physical systems'.

4 Lacking one of the three factors, the market can still allocate resources efficiently *vis-à-vis* the firm: 1) without bounded rationality, all future potential problems can be solved once and for all and opportunism and asset specificity can be managed by the market; 2) without opportunism, *stewardship* can be used to replace hierarchy (since the parties can rely on each other for respect of the commitments); 3) without asset specificity, contestable markets in Baumol's sense can be defined (cf. Pitelis 1991, p. 12).

5 The radical approach of Bowles and Gintis has been criticised for the deep change in perspective with respect to Marx's conception and for the implications on the scientific and political identity of the whole radical school by Baker and Weisbrot (1994), McIntyre and Hillard (1995), and Spencer (2000). Starting from the late 1990s, Bowles and Gintis have progressively abandoned this line of research based on 'contested exchange', distanced themselves from the radical school and redirected their scientific program towards behavioural sciences. Their theoretical evolution, however, is not a consequence of a process of methodological autocriticism but is rather an attempt to exploit new mathematical tools within the neoclassical framework.

6 Bowles and Gintis distinguish between 'perfect competition' and 'perfect Walrasian competition': the former does not imply market clearing, the latter does (and coincides with what in the literature is generally called 'perfect competition'). Ultimately, this is why they can claim that power relations exist even in the reign of perfect competition (with non-clearing markets). In this book, I will continue to adopt the definition of perfect competition as implying market clearing.

7 This process of inclusion of heterodox economics within the mainstream is part of a more general process of cultural hegemony of neoclassical economics within social sciences. Fine and Milonakis (2009) discuss in details the emergence of a sort of 'economics imperialism' based on methodological individualism, utility maximisation and market imperfections and the consequent desocialisation and dehistoricisation of political economy.

References

Akerlof, George and Janet Yallen (1986 eds), *Efficiency wage models of the labor market*, Cambridge, Cambridge University Press.

Alchian, Armen and Harold Demsetz (1972), Production, information costs and economic organization, *American Economic Review*, vol. 62, n. 1, pp. 777–95.

Ankarloo, Daniel and Giulio Palermo (2004), Anti-Williamson: A Marxian critique of new institutional economics, *Cambridge Journal of Economics*, vol. 28, n. 3, pp. 413–29.

Arrow, Kenneth (1969), The organization of economic activity: issues pertinent to the choice of market versus non-market allocation, in US Joint Committee, 91st Congress, 1st Session, *The analysis and evaluation of public expenditure: The PPB system*, Vol. 1, Washington DC, US Government Printing Office. Reprinted in Haveman, Robert and Julius Margolis (1970 eds), *Public expenditures and policy analysis*, Chicago, Markham.

Baker, Dean and Mark Weisbrot (1994), The logic of contested exchange, *Journal of Economic Issues*, vol. 28, n. 4, pp. 1091–114.

Becker, Gary (1992), Comments to Cheung, in Werin, Lars and Hans Wijkander (eds), *Contract economics*, Oxford, Basil Blackwell.

Bowles, Samuel (1985), The production process in a competitive economy: Walrasian, Marxian and neo-Hobbesian models, *American Economic Review*, vol. 75, pp. 16–36.

Bowles, Samuel, Maurizio Franzini and Ugo Pagano (2004 eds), *The politics and economics of power*, London, Routledge.

Bowles, Samuels and Herbert Gintis (1988), Contested exchange: political economy and modern economic theory, *American Economic Review*, vol. 78, pp. 145–50.

——(1990), Contested exchange: New microfoundations for the political economy of capitalism, *Politics and Society*, vol. 18, n. 2, pp. 165–222.

——(1993A), Power and wealth in a competitive capitalist economy, *Philosophy and Public Affairs*, vol. 21, n. 4, pp. 324–53.

——(1993B), The revenge of homo economicus: Contested exchange and the revival of political economy, *Journal of Economic Perspectives*, vol. 7, n. 1, pp. 83–102.

——(1993C), Post Walrasian political economy, in Bowles, Samuel, Herbert Gintis and Bo Gustafsson (eds), *Markets and democracy: Participation, accountability and efficiency*, Cambridge, Cambridge University Press.

——(1993D). The democratic firm: An agency-theoretic evaluation, in Bowles, Samuel, Herbert Gintis and Bo Gustafsson (eds), *Markets and democracy: Participation, accountability and efficiency*, Cambridge, Cambridge University Press.

——(1994A), Power in economic theory, in Philip Arestis and Malcolm Sawyer (eds), *The Elgar companion to radical political economy*, Aldershot, Edward Elgar.

——(1994B), Credit market imperfections and the incidence of worker-owned firms, *Metroeconomica*, vol. 45, n. 3, pp. 209–23.

——(2000), Walrasian economics in retrospect, *The Quarterly Journal of Economics*, vol. 115, n. 4, pp. 1411–39.

——(2012), Power, in Steven Durlauf and Lawrence Blume (eds), *The new Palgrave dictionary of economics*, Basingstoke, Palgrave Macmillan.

Bowles, Samuel, Herbert Gintis and Bo Gustafsson (1993 eds), *Markets and democracy: Participation, accountability and efficiency*, Cambridge, Cambridge University Press.

Braverman, Harry (1974), *Labour and monopoly capital: The degradation of work in the twentieth century*, New York, Monthly Review Press.

Cheung, Stephen (1983), The contractual nature of the firm, *Journal of Law and Economics*, vol. 26, n. 1, pp. 1–21.

——(1987), Economic organization and transaction costs, in Eatwell, John, Murray Millgate and Paul Newman (eds), *The new Palgrave: A dictionary of economics*, London, Macmillan.

——(1992), On the new institutional economics, in Werin, Lars and Hans Wijkander (eds), *Contract economics*, Oxford, Basil Blackwell.

Coase, Ronald (1937), The nature of the firm, *Economica*, vol. 4, n. 4, pp. 386–405.

——(1960), The problem of social cost, *Journal of Law and Economics*, n. 3, pp. 1–44.

Edwards, Richard (1979), *Contested terrain: The transformation of the workplace in the twentieth century*, New York, Basis Books.

Fine, Ben and Dimitris Milonakis (2009), *From economics imperialism to freakonomics: The shifting boundaries between economics and other social sciences*, London, Routledge.

Gintis, Herbert (1989), Financial markets and the political structure of the enterprise, *Journal of Economic Behavior and Organization*, vol. 11, pp. 311–22.

Gintis, Herbert and Tsuneo Ishikawa (1981), Wages, work discipline, and unemployment, *Journal of Japanese and International Economics*, vol. 1, pp. 195–228.

Goldberg, Victor (1976), Toward an expanded economic theory of contract, *Journal of Economic Issues*, vol. 10, n. 1, pp. 45–61.

——(1980), Bridges over contested terrain: Exploring the radical account of the employment relationship, *Journal of Economic Behavior and Organization*, vol. 1, pp. 249–74.

Granovetter, Mark (1985), Economic action and social structure: The problem of embeddedness, *Journal of American Sociology*, vol. 91, n. 3, pp. 481–510.

Greenwald, Bruce and Joseph Stiglitz (1988), Pareto inefficiency of market economies: Search and efficiency wage models, *American Economic Review*, vol. 78, n. 2, pp. 351–55.

——(1993), New and old Keynesians, *Journal of Economic Perspectives*, vol. 7, n. 1, pp. 23–44.

Grossman, Stanford and Oliver Hart (1983), An Analysis of the principal-agent problem, *Econometrica*, vol. 51, pp. 7–45.

——(1986), The costs and benefits of ownership: A theory of vertical and lateral integration. *Journal of Political Economy*, vol. 94, n. 4, pp. 691–719.

Hart, Oliver (1988), Incomplete contracts and the theory of the firm, *Journal of Law, Economics and Organization*, vol. 4, n. 1, pp. 119–40.

——(1989), An economist's perspective on the theory of the firm, *Columbia Law Review*, vol. 89, n. 7, pp. 1757–74.

——(1990), Is bounded rationality an important element of a theory of institutions?, *Journal of Institutional and Theoretical Economics*, vol. 146, n. 4, pp. 696–702.

——(1995), *Firms, contracts and financial structure*, Oxford, Clarendon.

——(1996), An economist's view of authority, *Rationality and Society*, vol. 8, pp. 371–86.

Hart, Oliver and John Moore (1988), Incomplete contracts and renegotiation, *Econometrica*, vol. 56, pp. 755–85.

——(1990), Property rights and the nature of the firm, *Journal of Political Economy*, vol. 98, n. 6, pp. 1119–58.

——(2005), On the design of hierarchies: Coordination versus specialization, *Journal of Political Economy*, vol. 113, n. 4, pp. 675–702.

——(2007), Incomplete contracts and ownership: Some new thoughts, *American Economic Review*, vol. 97, n. 2, pp. 182–86.

——(2008), Contracts as reference points, *Quarterly Journal of Economics*, vol. 123, n. 1, pp. 1–48.

Hodgson, Geoffrey (1988), *Economics and institutions*, Cambridge, Polity Press.

——(1991), Economic evolution, intervention contra Pangloss, *Journal of Economic Issues*, vol. 25, n. 2.

——(1993A), *Economics and evolution: Bringing life back into economics*, Cambridge, Polity Press.

——(1993B), Transaction costs and the evolution of the firm, in Pitelis, Christos (ed.), *Transaction costs, markets and hierarchies*, Oxford, Basil Blackwell.

——(1994), Evolution and optimality, in Hodgson, Geoffrey, Warren Samuels and Marc Tool (eds), *The Elgar companion to institutional and evolutionary economics*, Aldershot, Edward Elgar.

Jensen, Michael and William Meckling (1976), Theory of the firm: Managerial behaviour, agency costs and ownership structure, *Journal of Financial Economics*, n. 3, pp. 305–60.

Marglin, Stephen (1974), What do bosses do? The origins and functions of hierarchy in capitalist production, Part 1, *Review of Radical Political Economics*, vol. 6, n. 2, pp. 60–112.

——(1975), What do bosses do? The origins and functions of hierarchy in capitalist production, Part 2, *Review of Radical Political Economics*, vol. 7, n. 1, pp. 20–37.

——(1991), Understanding capitalism: Control versus efficiency, in Gustavsson, Bo (ed.), *Power and economic institutions*, Aldershot, Edward Elgar.

Marx, Karl (1867), *Capital: Critique of political economy, vol, 1, The process of capitalist production*. Retrieved from www.marxists.org/archive/marx/works/1867-c1/index.htm (accessed 1 March 2016).

McIntyre, Richard and Michael Hillard (1995), The peculiar marriage of Marxian and neoclassical labor economics, *Review of Radical Political Economics*, vol. 27, pp. 22–30.

Moore, John (1992), The firm as a collection of assets, *European Economic Review*, vol. 36, n. 2/3, pp. 493–507.

Palermo, Giulio (2000), Economic power and the firm: Two conflicting problems, *Journal of Economic Issues*, vol. 34, n. 3, pp. 573–601.

Pitelis, Christos (1991), *Market and non-market hierarchies: Theories of institutional failure*, Oxford, Basil Blackwell.

Putterman, Louis (1982), Some behavioral perspectives on the dominance of hierarchical over democratic forms of enterprise, *Journal of Economic Behavior and Organization*, vol. 3, pp. 139–60.

——(1984), On some recent explanations of why capital hires labor, *Economic Inquiry*, vol. 22, pp. 171–87.

——(1993), Ownership and the nature of the firm, *Journal of Comparative Economics*, vol. 17, pp. 243–63.

——(1995), Markets, hierarchies and information: On a paradox in the economics of organization, *Journal of Economic Behavior and Organization*, vol. 26, pp. 373–90.

Samuelson, Paul (1957), Wage and interest: A modern dissection of Marxian economic models, *American Economic Review*, vol. 47, pp. 884–912.

Screpanti, Ernesto (2001), *The fundamental institutions of capitalism*, London, Routledge.

Shapiro, Carl and Joseph Stiglitz (1984), Equilibrium unemployment as a worker discipline device, *American Economic Review*, vol. 74, n. 3, pp. 433–44.

Simon, Herbert (1951), A formal theory of the employment relationship, *Econometrica*, vol. 19, n. 3, pp. 293–305.

——(1991), Organizations and markets, *Journal of Economic Perspectives*, vol. 5, pp. 25–44.

Spencer, David (2000), The demise of radical political economics? An essay on the evolution of a theory of capitalist production, *Cambridge Journal of Economics*, vol. 24, pp 543–64.

Williamson, Oliver (1975), *Markets and hierarchies: Analysis and antitrust implications: A study in the economics of internal organization*, New York, Free Press.

——(1985), *The economic institutions of capitalism: Firms, markets, relational contracting*, New York, Free Press.

——(1994), Visible and invisible governance, *American Economic Review, Papers and Proceedings*, vol. 84, n. 2, pp. 323–6.

——(1995), Hierarchies, markets and power in the economy: An economic perspective, *Industrial and Corporate Change*, vol. 4, n. 1, pp. 21–49.

——(1996A), *The mechanisms of governance*, Oxford, Oxford University Press.

——(1996B), Efficiency, power, authority and economic organization, in Groenewegen, John (ed.), *Transaction costs economics and beyond*, London, Kluwer Academic Publishers.

——(2003), Examining economic organization through the lens of contract, *Industrial and Corporate Change*, vol. 12, n. 4, pp. 917–42.

——(2005), The economics of governance, *American Economic Review*, vol. 95, pp. 1–18.

Williamson, Oliver and William Ouchi (1983), The market and hierarchies program of research: Origins, implications, prospects, in Francis, Arthur, Jeremy Turk and Paul Willman, (eds), *Power, efficiency and institutions*, London, Heinemann.

3 Power and post Walrasian economics

> The neoclassical market is an act of God, not an act of man. It is natural rather than artificial. ... It is not a unit of enquiry, something to be investigated. Instead it is something to be assumed, taken for granted. ... It is viewed as a self-generated phenomenon, a product of immaculate conception and virgin birth.
>
> (Dugger 1992, p. 89)

As we have seen, the debate on power leads to an ontology in which power and perfect competition are disjoint empirical sets: where there is one, there is not the other. Theoretically, in this conception, power and competition are perfectly symmetrical. The debate, however, has focused only on the nature of power relations, whereas competition has been taken for granted, as a natural condition, which deserves no theoretical explanation. In this approach, power is the *explanandum*, competition is part of the *explanans*.

The assumption of perfect competition as a starting point for the explanation of power goes hand in hand with the introduction of imperfections in the DMC. More precisely, the general attempt to explain power by means of imperfections is a consequence of this assumption. In this chapter, I argue that both the assumption of perfect competition and the introduction of imperfections have no theoretical justification.

I begin by collocating the debate on power within the broader research program developed by the so called 'post Walrasian economics'.[1]

Then, I discuss the relationship between Walrasian and post Walrasian economics. First, I show that logically power relations do not depend on imperfections. My argument is counterfactual: I assume the perfect DMC and show that OSs based on power relations have the same theoretical legitimacy as the Walrasian one, based on perfect competition. This means that imperfections are not a theoretical necessity and that, conceptually, perfect competition has no special role to play in this approach.

Second, I argue that, paradoxically, the explanatory method of post Walrasian economics does not take into account the theoretical results reached by Walrasian economics: the problems of stability and uniqueness of a general equilibrium are simply neglected, the role of existence and Pareto optimality are misinterpreted and market failures are ruled out by assumptions. This leads to a mystified conception of both power and perfect competition, the former as caused by imperfections, the latter as a pre-existing state of nature.

My critique continues by discussing the role of this pre-existing perfectly decentralised OS in the different approaches to power. As in the previous chapter, I have discussed the terms of the debate on power by looking at the role of perfect and imperfect DMCs, here I develop my critique by discussing also the role of perfectly and imperfectly decentralised OS.

Finally, I synthesise the main theoretical results and the logical contradictions of this approach.

Post Walrasian economics

Methodologically, the debate on power is a sort of general comparative exercise between OSs operating within imperfect DMCs. The starting point is always the same: the Walrasian (perfectly competitive, completely decentralised) OS in the perfect DMC. This is the explicit or implicit theoretical benchmark of all these exercises.

The analysis of this benchmark began in the 1870s with the formalisation of the general equilibrium model by Léon Walras (1874) and Vilfredo Pareto (1897) and continued for decades, before leading, in the 1950s, to Kenneth Arrow and Gérard Debreu's solutions of the problem of existence and Pareto optimality of a general equilibrium (Arrow and Debreu 1954, Debreu 1959, Arrow and Hahn 1971) and, in the 1970s, to Sonneschein-Mantel-Debreu's impossibility theorem on stability and uniqueness (Sonnenschein 1973, Debreu 1974, Mantel 1974).[2]

Paradoxically, it is only at this point – when Walrasian economics had arrived at maturity and perhaps at senility – that power enters formally the scene. Whilst serious general equilibrium theorists largely recognise the consequences of the negative results on stability and uniqueness on the general coherence and interpretative power of this research program (cf. Hahn 1982, Fisher 2011), post Walrasian economists start building a new research program on these fragile bases.

As we have seen, power is formally introduced in this theoretical framework by relaxing the assumptions of the perfect DMC. This attempt to develop Walrasian economics within imperfect DMCs is not a methodological specificity of the debate on power. It is rather the general method followed by the so called 'post Walrasian economics' to deal with the set of problems that cannot be discussed within the original Walrasian model and that were generally developed by heterodox schools. The logic is the following. In the perfect DMC, Walrasian economics has reached the following results:

1 The state has no economic role to play, since resources allocation can occur entirely through the market.
2 There is no economic room for the firm, since production can be carried out by interpersonal contracts, without managerial coordination.
3 There exists no power relation in market interaction since perfect competition alone may govern interpersonal relations.

The common idea of new Keynesians, new institutionalists and neoclassical radicals is to explain the economic role of the state, the nature of the firm (and, more generally, of capitalist institutions) and the existence of power relations by modifying the assumptions of the Walrasian DMC. Methodologically, these new approaches can thus be seen as part of a common research program, aiming at extending and generalising the Walrasian framework: the latter assumes a perfect DMC; post Walrasian economics investigates 'imperfect' DMCs.

The explanatory logic of this approach is based on the assumption that institutional evolution is guided by Pareto improvements. It can be described as follows: when the conditions of the real world approach the perfect DMC, the perfectly competitive OS – the initial, pre-existing, OS – will approach Pareto optimality and will tend to prevail in the real world. Only with imperfect DMCs, the Walrasian OS fails and only in this case, according to this approach, there is room for power-based OSs (to the extent that they reduce Pareto sub-optimalities). The mixed OSs of real capitalist economies might then be interpreted as institutional solutions to the inefficiency produced by the existence of imperfections in the DMC.

Methodologically, this is a way to establish a causal relation between the features of the DMC and the evolution of the OS. According to this logic, the state, the firm and power relations have a reason to exist only to the extent that they provide economically superior results with respect to pre-existing perfectly competitive markets.

In winter 1993, the editors of the *Journal of economic perspectives* have solicited some authoritative exponents of this broad research program, including Stiglitz (1993), Williamson (1993) and Bowles and Gintis (1993B), to present their 'new' theoretical approaches and discuss both the relationships among them and those with the founding authors of their respective old schools: John Maynard Keynes, American institutionalists and Marx. The picture that emerges is that, notwithstanding their different focuses, there exists a common methodological and theoretical ground among these approaches, which makes them largely compatible with each other and with mainstream neoclassical economics (despite the fact that a synthesis between Keynesianism, institutionalism and Marxism has proven to be a much more problematic issue): methodological individualism, equilibrium and comparative statics define the general framework underlying this process of convergence; imperfections are the theoretical ingredients to overcome the restrictive assumptions of the Walrasian model. With this methodological and theoretical characterisation, the whole debate on power is in fact part of the research program of post Walrasian economics.

From Walrasian to post Walrasian economics

The first thing to notice is that the assumption of a Walrasian OS as theoretical benchmark is a purely ideological choice.

Logically, there are three ways to introduce power relations in the Walrasian framework: 1) by rejecting the Walrasian OS, 2) by rejecting the perfect DMC or 3) by rejecting both of them. Without any theoretical reason, however, the first possibility (a power-based OS defined in the perfect DMC) has been completely neglected by post Walrasians and the debate on power has developed only along the second and the third ways. Before problematising the DMC, however, post Walrasians might study power in the perfect DMC, exactly as Walrasians did with perfect competition.

In principle, any OS can be defined within any DMC. For instance, in the same perfect DMC of the Walrasian model, it is possible to define a central planning model, based on purely hierarchical relations, or even OSs with intermediate degrees of centralisation, such as multi-planning models, based on both competition and power relations. Power relations are thus absolutely compatible with the perfect DMC, and their existence is not subordinated to the existence of imperfections in the empirical realm. Theoretically, the assumption of the perfect DMC does not imply that 1) the market should be the sole allocative mechanism, 2) production should occur through bilateral contracts and 3) interpersonal relations should be regulated by perfect competition, as post Walrasian economics suggests. These are only possibilities, not necessities.

Clearly, by assuming an OS based on power, the latter remains unexplained, as being a pure assumption (exactly as Walras assumed competition without explaining it). The effects of power and competition might then be compared on the ground of Pareto optimality or other criteria but their causes will remain external to the model. In other words, competition and power have exactly the same theoretical status in the perfect DMC: both of them can be coherently assumed, but obviously what is assumed cannot be explained.

The fact that power relations exist in reality but are absent in the Walrasian model does not imply that the perfect DMC is inadequate. It proves rather that the Walrasian model is not the best starting point to shed light on power-related issues. But the problem might be as much in its DMC as in its OS. Rather than problematising the DMC, power may be studied by introducing it explicitly in the OS. The fact that all authors reject the perfect DMC, but keep the Walrasian OS, is not a theoretical necessity in this approach. It is rather part of the phenomenon to explain. Its cause is not in the explanatory method of post Walrasian economics but in the mystified conception of perfect competition inherited from Walrasian economics, a conception in which competition is assumed as a natural condition, whereas all other forms of social interaction need to be explained.

In this research program, the introduction of imperfections in the DMC and the transformation of the Walrasian OS into a natural pre-existing OS are parts of the same mystifying process. Their cause is not in economic theory but in bourgeois ideology.

The theoretical results of Walrasian economics

A second problematic aspect of the relationship between Walrasian and post Walrasian economics regards the theoretical results obtained by the former. There are three main problems to discuss: the results on stability and uniqueness of a general equilibrium, the role of existence and Pareto optimality and the role of market failures.

Stability and uniqueness of a general equilibrium

As I have already mentioned, post Walrasian economics develops its interpretative framework as if the negative results concerning stability and uniqueness in the Walrasian model did not occur. However, with possibly unstable and multiple equilibria the whole explanatory logic of this approach – based on comparative statics – becomes problematic. Technically, we can always compare equilibrium points but, theoretically, there is no reason to expect that the real system will actually move from one equilibrium to another if the latter is not an attractor for the system. And if also the former equilibrium is unstable, there is neither any reason to assume that the actual system was in fact in the initial position of this hypothetical process. Finally, in case of multiple equilibria, we do not even know which equilibrium position should represent the actual economy and towards which equilibrium it should converge.

Unfortunately, the impossibility to exclude unstable and multiple equilibria is precisely the result of the Sonneschein-Mantel-Debreu's impossibility theorem: with the assumptions of the Walrasian model, the general equilibrium might be stable or unstable, unique or not unique. All cases are possible.

In the next chapter, I will criticise the use of comparative statics as method to explain real evolutionary processes. Here, however, we have an internal problem within neoclassical economics. With unstable or multiple equilibria, comparative statics is simply inappropriate to describe historical processes and to shed light on real economic phenomena.

From the outset, the post Walrasian approach incorporates thus an internal contradiction. It wishes to develop and generalise Walrasian economics, but in fact it neglects the theoretical *impasse* of the latter. While Walrasians search in all ways how to overcome their theoretical problems on stability and uniqueness, post Walrasians take Walrasian economics as methodological foundation of their broader research program.[3]

Existence and Pareto optimality

Paradoxically, post Walrasian economics misinterprets also the positive results of Walrasian economics concerning existence and Pareto optimality of a general equilibrium. To isolate the consequences of this problem, let us assume that a general equilibrium is stable and unique (there is no guarantee that this occurs under general conditions, yet it is a theoretical possibility). In this case, the transition from one equilibrium point to another might be interpreted as a march towards Pareto improvements, like post Walrasian economics suggests: as soon as the complexity of the DMC makes one equilibrium suboptimal, the system will indeed move towards a Pareto superior equilibrium.

Somehow, this logic attempts to justify the special role played by the Walrasian OS in the post Walrasian framework. Indeed, its Pareto optimality in the perfect DMC explains – according to post Walrasians – why it exists in real empirical context without imperfections and why it might be a good starting point in comparative statics exercises within imperfect DMCs. If this argument worked, then the choice of an initial Walrasian OS would not be grounded merely on ideology but on the results of economic theory.

This explanatory logic, however, is the product of a false syllogism. The Walrasian OS, in fact, is not the only Pareto optimal OS in the perfect DMC. A well-known theoretical result is that, a model of perfect planning, with purely hierarchical relations, defined in a perfect DMC and formalised by the convex programming model, is compatible with Pareto optimality as well (Kantorovich 1939, 1965, Koopmans 1951 ed., 1960). The equivalency of these two OSs based on perfect competition and perfect authority can also be generalised to OSs with intermediate degrees of centralisation (such as OSs based on firms and market relations) as soon as one notices that shadow prices in the planning model can be used as signals for decentralised entrepreneurs in a multi-level planning OS, with hierarchical relations between the central planner and decentralised entrepreneurs, and competitive relations among the latter.

The role of planning models – both in the perfect DMC and in imperfect DMCs – has not passed unnoticed in economic literature, as proven by the Nobel prizes awarded to the mathematical economists that have developed them.[4] Unfortunately, however, these models have played no role in the debate on power and within post Walrasian economics at large. In post Walrasian economics, the Pareto efficiency of other OSs is ignored and the Walrasian OS is simply assumed as a natural fact, both in the perfect DMC and in imperfect DMCs, that's it.

However, if we really follow the post Walrasian idea that OSs evolve according to Pareto movements, planning models show that we might coherently expect to observe both power-based and power-free OSs already in the perfect DMC. Therefore, even by following this evolutionary logic based on Pareto efficiency, there is no reason to introduce imperfections in order to explain the existence of power-based OSs in the real world.

In the perfect DMC, perfect competition has no special role to play, not even as a theoretical starting point for comparative exercises. In this evolutionary logic, if one mode of social interaction appears first, no other mode should arise. Competition and power can both be assumed as starting points, but they cannot be explained as results of institutional evolution. Therefore, the problem of the nature of power and competition should either not be posed at all (since their existence must be assumed and cannot be explained), or else it should be posed for both of them (since they are theoretically symmetrical, each one being redundant as soon as the other is assumed).

Market failures

Contrary to what we have conceded until now, central planning and perfect competition are not really equivalent in the perfect DMC. If the Walrasian OS is Pareto optimal in the perfect DMC, it is only because all potential causes of 'market failures' (market allocations that are not Pareto optimal) have been eliminated from the Walrasian model by assumption.

For instance, with increasing returns to scale (which can hardly be considered a rarity in the real world) competitive markets fail (whereas central planning does not). In this case, the Walrasian OS is incompatible with Pareto efficiency in the perfect DMC and, according to the evolutionary conception of this approach, it should never be observed in the real world: indeed, if it accidentally came into existence, it would be immediately superseded by Pareto superior forms of planning.

Therefore, if one really follows this explanatory method, it would be more reasonable to start from a centrally planned OS, rather than from a Walrasian one. And if, according to this logic, imperfections have truly something to explain, it should be competition, not power.

The role of perfect competition in the debate on power

The perfectly competitive OS plays a central role within the entire debate on power. Post Walrasian economists, however, have accorded it two different roles, either as a real entity or as an only theoretical benchmark. In one case, it has been considered simply as an adequate representation of contemporary capitalism. On this issue, there is a curious convergence between the opposite radicalisms of Alchian and Demsetz, on the one hand, and Bowles and Gintis, on the other, both equally convinced of the realism of the Walrasian OS. New institutionalists, such as Coase and Williamson, or Hart and Moore, follow instead a different path. In their view, modern capitalist economies are better represented by mixed OSs, based on both competition and hierarchical relations. They preserve however a special role for the Walrasian OS as a theoretical reference and as a starting point for the explanation of non-Walrasian OSs. Let me consider these theoretical positions in more details.

Table 3.1 Power, decision making contexts and organisational structures

	Perfectly decentralised OS	*Centralised OSs*
Perfect DMC	General equilibrium model (Arrow-Debreu)	Planning theory (Kantorovich, Koopmans)
Imperfect DMCs	Contractualism, Radical political economics (Alchian-Demsetz, Bowles-Gintis)	New institutionalism (Coase-Williamson, Hart-Moore)

The general assumption is that the general equilibrium model, with its perfect DMC and perfectly decentralised OS, leaves no room for power relations.

Alchian and Demsetz's and Bowles and Gintis' opposite forms of radicalism are both based on the assumption that the Walrasian OS adequately describes real capitalist systems. In their view, the problem of the general equilibrium model is not in the OS, but in the DMC – too aseptic to describe real decision making processes within modern capitalism. As Bowles and Gintis (1993B, p. 83) put it, standard Walrasian theory 'depicts a charmingly Victorian but utopian world in which conflicts abound but a handshake is a handshake'. In such a world, all human relations are regulated by private contracts, but contract enforcement problems do not really exist, or, as the two radical economists say, are regulated by a simple handshake. They thus keep the perfectly competitive OS of the Walrasian model, but question the realism of the perfect DMC. Similarly, Alchian and Demsetz introduce imperfect information in order to explain the firm, but, at the same time, describe the firm as a form of perfectly competitive market, exactly as in the Walrasian OS.

Where the two approaches diverge is in their interpretation of the resulting model of perfect competition within an imperfect DMC. Alchian and Demsetz contend that perfect (Walrasian) competition regulates interpersonal relations even within the firm. This, in their view, rules out any possible power relation from the economy. As we have seen, however, this position is theoretically inconsistent since it presupposes that market relations are necessarily power-free. Bowles and Gintis, by contrast, demonstrate that, in an imperfect DMC, even perfect competition (in non-clearing markets) necessarily involves power.

It is noteworthy that neither Alchian and Demsetz, nor Bowles and Gintis engage in any defence of the realism of the perfectly competitive OS. They all identify capitalism with a highly decentralised system based on competitive relations, and do not provide any evidence that capitalism, somewhere, in some epoch, did in fact resemble a decentralised model. Bowles and Gintis write:

> Of course, if economic conditions in advanced capitalist countries deviated sufficiently from the norms of free entry and exit to account for the observed incidence of economic power, the need for an alternative account would be unnecessary. We do not believe this is the case.
>
> (Bowles and Gintis 1993A, p. 328, note 14)

They do not believe this is the case. This is the argument. Empirical evidence that free entry and exit are not the norm, however, is abundant. Within Marxism and other critical perspectives, this issue has been developed for more than a century under the rubric of imperialism. But the monopolisation of the economy is by now a fact recognised also by major international organisations. For instance, at the US progressive think tank *Institute for policy studies*, Sarah Anderson, John Cavanagh and Thea Lee (2005) show that, if by 'economy' we mean both a corporation and a country, of the 100 largest economies in the world, 51 are corporations and only 49 are countries. This should cast some doubts on the assumption that the OS of modern capitalist economies has something in common with the Walrasian one.

New institutional authors follow a slightly different path. They too start from the perfectly competitive OS ('in the beginning there were markets', says Williamson), but rather than remaining attached to it, they 'explain' how it 'evolves', according to the features of the DMC. Of course, this process of evolution does not occur in the real history of capitalism, but only in the mind of the economist. In this conception, the Walrasian OS is not a real entity, but a theoretical one. Different from left and right radicals, new institutional economists thus question the realism of the Walrasian OS, and try to explain how mixed OSs might have come into existence, as the evolutionary product of such a hypothetical starting point.

Faced with the equivalency results holding in the perfect DMC between centralised and decentralised OSs, new institutional economists distance themselves from the perfect DMC. The Walrasian OS remains an ideal starting point, but is not at all necessary theoretically. Having introduced imperfections in the DMC, competition and power can now be explained as optimal solutions to specific allocation problems. In the perfect DMC, equivalency results made this methodology insufficient to univocally determine an optimal OS. In the imperfect DMCs of new institutional economics, by contrast, general equivalency theorems do not hold, and the existing OS (with its forms of power and competition) can thus be explained by means of exercises in comparative statics, provided that one initial mode of interaction is assumed to pre-exist. Of course, comparative statics assures that the 'final' OS does not depend on initial conditions. But the question remains: now that we have left the perfect DMC, why start from a system of complete markets and perfect competition and not, for instance, from the planning state and perfect authority?

Clearly the answer to this question cannot be sought in the perfect DMC, since, as we have seen, within such a context, the Walrasian OS has no special role to play (and, to be rigorous, with market failures, it is not even a legitimate candidate to be a theoretical starting point, since centrally planned OSs are economically superior). The curious thing, however, is that even within new institutional economics nobody starts from central planning or other power-based OSs and, like other post Walrasians, all agree that it is more 'convenient' to assume that 'in the beginning there were markets'.

Methodologically, this special role accorded to perfect competition creates a twofold problem: first, by assuming the existence of one primordial institution and one primordial mode of interaction, post Walrasians refrain from explaining them and thus treat them as universal; second, by identifying this starting point with the system of perfectly competitive markets, they inevitably fall into a sterile idealisation of this institution and of its mode of functioning. Had they assumed an initial starting point of pure planning, with rigid authoritarian relations, or one of a mixed institutional set-up with different forms of power, they would have been more coherent with their method (in the sense that perfect planning is superior to perfect competition). Yet they would have been unable to explain these institutions of capitalism and their internal power relations, therefore the project would have been contradictory anyway.

But the choice of perfect competition as a natural predefined OS is also apologetic, since it transforms the market from a historical institution into a universal category. William Dugger (1992, p. 89) is trenchant:

> The neoclassical market is an act of God, not an act of man. It is natural rather than artificial. ... The natural market is beyond the will of humans. It is a product of nature existing outside of history. ... But the spontaneous market, the natural market, is an assumption. It is not a unit of enquiry, something to be investigated. Instead it is something to be assumed, taken for granted. ... The market is taken as the only real circulation process and the market is simply assumed to exist. It is viewed as a self-generated phenomenon, a product of immaculate conception and virgin birth.

Competition in this conception is not a mode of social interaction that developed historically, but a universal category, existing outside of history.

Conclusions

Apparently, the post Walrasian logic is straightforward. In the Walrasian model – defined in the perfect DMC – there is no room for power relations. This contradicts everyday life. The causes of power must then be sought out of the perfect DMC. This logic, however, is untenable.

First, in a static framework, like the Walrasian one, it is possible to define power-based OSs, without introducing imperfections. Therefore, logically, 1) there is no reason to reject the perfect DMC in order to study power relations and 2) there is no reason to accord a special role to the perfectly competitive OS in the perfect DMC. Any possible OS – based on pure competition, pure power relations or both of them – might be assumed, but none of them can be explained in this theoretical framework.

Second, in an evolutionary framework, like that of post Walrasian economics, the negative results on uniqueness and stability of a general equilibrium make the use of comparative statics contradictory. This casts doubts on the whole explanatory logic of this approach.

Third, in the perfect DMC, there are some equivalency theorems, which show that the Walrasian OS is not the only one to be compatible with Pareto optimality. There is thus no theoretical reason to assume an initial Walrasian OS in these comparative statics exercises. *In the beginning there were markets* is an ideological statement, without theoretical justification. In this theoretical framework, any Pareto optimal OS might be a coherent starting point.

Fourth, at a closer inspection, the existence of market failures in the perfect DMC shows that the Walrasian OS is not only unnecessary but even impossible. *In the beginning there were markets* is a contradiction in terms: if accidentally a system of pure markets came into existence, in this evolutionary logic, it would rapidly be superseded by economically superior OSs. To be rigorous, in the post Walrasian framework, *in the beginning there were hierarchies and central planning* (the only OSs compatible with Pareto optimality) are the only coherent starting points.

In sum, post Walrasian economics is a mix of wrong hypotheses and weak logical-deductive rigour. This is the price these authors are ready to pay in order to provide a picture of the existing power relations as Pareto optimal solutions to preconceived allocative problems.

These theoretical critiques are all internal to neoclassical economics. They show that post Walrasian economics falls on its own contradictions. It erects a skyscraper over a crumbling building and it does it when the building has already been condemned. Rather than enlarging the explanatory framework of Walrasian economics, this approach enlarges its contradictions. Post Walrasian economics develops Walrasian economics by simply ignoring its theoretical *cul-de-sac*.

These theoretical contradictions help us understanding the ideological bias of this research program. Indirectly, they also shed light on the reasons why post Walrasians see the problem of power this way. But to fully grasp the mystified conception of power developed by these economists we must now move from the theoretical critique to a meta-theoretical one and discuss the methodology, ontology and ideology of this approach.

Notes

1   In a narrower sense, the term post Walrasian economics is used also as a synonymous of the radical approach to power started by Bowles and Gintis.
2   The proof of existence of a general equilibrium was anticipated by McKenzie (1954). The main differences with respect to Arrow and Debreu (1954) is that 1) McKenzie does not start with individual preferences and endowments but with aggregate demand functions and 2) he does not discuss Pareto optimality. The different academic fortunes of the articles by Arrow and Debreu and by McKenzie are discussed by Weintraub (2011).

3 The main research lines within Walrasian economics after the Sonneschein-Mantel-Debreu theorem are discussed by Rizvi (2006).
4 Planning models have developed as applications of linear programming (then generalised as convex programming), first discovered in 1939 by the Soviet mathematician and economist Leonid Vitalevic Kantorovich, who also understood its applicability at the levels of industrial and national resource allocation. For his results, Kantorovich was rewarded by the Lenin prize in 1965 (one of the most prestigious awards in Soviet union) and by the Nobel prize in 1975 (shared with the American economist Tjalling Charles Koopmans, who arrived at the same mathematical technique some ten years later with an independent research path, financed by the *American Air force* and the *Rand corporation*).

References

Anderson, Sarah, John Cavanagh and Thea Lee (2005), *Field guide to the global economy,* New York, The New Press.

Arrow, Kenneth and Gérard Debreu (1954), Existence of equilibrium for a competitive economy, *Econometrica*, vol. 22, pp. 265–90.

Arrow, Kenneth and Frank Hahn (1971), *General competitive analysis,* San Francisco, Holden-Day.

Bowles, Samuels and Herbert Gintis (1993A), Power and wealth in a competitive capitalist economy, *Philosophy and Public Affairs*, vol. 21, n. 4, pp. 324–53.

——(1993B), The revenge of homo economicus: Contested exchange and the revival of political economy, *Journal of Economic Perspectives*, vol. 7, n. 1, pp. 83–102.

Debreu, Gérard (1959), *Theory of value*, London, Yale University Press.

——(1974), Excess demand functions, *Journal of Mathematical Economics*, vol. 1, pp. 15–23.

Dugger, William (1992), An evolutionary theory of the state and the market, in Dugger, William and William Waller (eds), *The stratified state: Radical institutionalist theories of participation and duality*, London, M. E. Sharp.

Fisher, Franklin (2011), The stability of general equilibrium – What do we know and why is it important?, in Bridel, Pascal (ed.), *General equilibrium analysis: A century after Walras*, London, Routledge.

Hahn, Frank (1982), Stability, in Arrow, Kenneth and Michael Intriligator (eds), *The handbook of mathematical economics, vol. II*, Amsterdam, North Holland.

Kantorovich, Leonid (1939), *Mathematicheskiye metody organizatsiyii planirovaniya proizvodstva*, Leningrad, Leningrad State University Press. English translation (1960): Mathematical methods of organizing and planning production, *Management Science*, vol. 6, n. 4, pp. 366–422.

——(1965), *The best use of economic resources*, Oxford, Pergamon Press.

Koopmans, Tjalling (1951 ed.), *Activity analysis of production and allocation*, New York, John Wiley and Sons.

——(1960), A note about Kantorovich's paper 'Mathematic methods of organizing and planning production', *Management Science*, vol. 6, n. 4, pp. 363–5.

Mantel, Rolf (1974), On the characterization of aggregate excess demand, *Journal of Economic Theory*, vol. 7, pp. 348–53.

McKenzie, Lionel (1954), On equilibrium in Graham's model of world trade and other competitive systems, *Econometrica*, vol. 22, pp. 147–61.

Pareto, Vilfredo (1896–7), *Cours d'economie politique professé à l'université de Lausanne, 2 tomes*, Lausanne, F. Rouge. English translation (1971): *Manual of political economy*, New York, August M. Kelley.

Rizvi, S. Abu Turab (2006), The Sonnenschein-Mantel-Debreu results after thirty years, *History of Political Economy*, vol. 38, pp. 228–45.

Sonnenschein, Hugo (1973), Do Walras' identity and continuity characterize the class of community excess demand functions?, *Journal of Economic Theory*, vol. 6, pp. 345–54.

Stiglitz, Joseph (1993), Post Walrasian and post Marxian economics, *Journal of Economic Perspectives*, vol. 7, n. 1, pp. 109–114.

Walras, Léon (1874), *Éléments d'économie politique pure, ou théorie de la richesse sociale*, Paris, R. Pichon and R. Durand-Auzias. English translation (2003): *Elements of pure economics: Or the theory of social wealth*, London, Routledge.

Weintraub, Roy (2011), Lionel W. McKenzie and the proof of the existence of a competitive equilibrium, *Journal of Economic Perspectives*, vol. 25, n. 2, pp. 199–215.

Williamson, Oliver (1993), Contested exchange versus the governance of contractual relations, *Journal of Economic Perspectives*, vol. 7, n. 1, pp. 103–8.

4 Power demystification

> I assume, for expositional convenience, that in the beginning there were markets.
>
> (Williamson 1975, p. 21)

> Do not let us go back to a fictitious primordial condition as the political economist does, when he tries to explain. Such a primordial condition explains nothing. He merely pushes the question away into a grey nebulous distance. He assumes in the form of fact, of an event, what he is supposed to deduce ... Theology in the same way explains the origin of evil by the fall of man: that is, it assumes as a fact, in historical form, what has to be explained.
>
> (Marx 1844, ch. 4)

In this chapter, I discuss the methodology of post Walrasian economics, the ontology that it presupposes and the ideology that inspires it. As a development of Walrasian economics, the methodology, ontology and ideology of post Walrasian economics incorporate the same methodological, ontological and ideological assumptions of the Walrasian model. My critique focuses on the way post Walrasian economics develops these assumptions into a mystified conception of power.

I begin with methodology. In order to answer its own scientific questions – which are derived from, but do not coincide with, those of Walras – post Walrasian economics introduces two new explanatory categories: imperfections and opportunism. Then, I criticise the comparative statics method as mode of explanation of real historical processes. I focus in particular on Williamson, who has explicitly developed his market-hierarchies framework as a tool to explain institutional evolution, and I discuss the general attempt of post Walrasian authors to interpret the actual institutional configuration as the product of an imaginary process towards Pareto optimality.

Walrasian methodology presupposes a particular ontology. From a Marxist viewpoint, this ontology is problematic for it is insufficient to characterise the capitalist mode of production. The problem is twofold: firstly, it assumes that capitalism coincides with free contracting; secondly, it conflates the spheres of production and circulation. Although post Walrasian economics does not develop any explicit ontological reasoning, its specific methodology based on imperfections imposes new conditions on this ontology. My critique therefore continues by discussing how this twofold problem inherited from Walrasian economics presents itself in the more sophisticated ontology of post Walrasian economics.

Here ends my 'scientific critique'. My work of demystification however continues with the discussion of the pre-scientific elements that lead post Walrasian economists to define their scientific problem. In an academic conception of science, the choice of the scientific problem is not generally an object of criticism: researchers are supposed to choose freely their scientific problems and are not called to defend these choices. Within post Walrasian economics, however, the acceptance of a common ideology and the definition of an identical scientific problem by all of its members – spanning from ultra-liberal to radical thinkers – are parts of the phenomenon to explain and must then be scrutinised critically.

The categories of post Walrasian economics

Methodologically, imperfections and opportunism are the essential ingredients for a power relation to exist. Both these categories are defined a-historically. The outcome is an a-historical conception of power totally detached from the real forms of coercion that characterise capitalism. Let me consider these explanatory categories more carefully.

Imperfections

Bounded rationality, imperfect information, historical time, etcetera are not historically specific to capitalism; rather, they are features of all human relations in any historical context. Clearly, rationality principles and imperfections change in the history of human societies, but each society has its imperfections, degrees of uncertainty, asymmetric information, irreversible phenomena, etcetera. Therefore, according to the post Walrasian logic, power relations exist in all social systems, since their cause – imperfections – are ubiquitous.

It is not the time to discuss whether this statement is right or wrong. For instance, in the Marxist tradition, all societies based on a certain division of labour and a degree of specialisation of their members are considered to be necessarily based on power relations. The methodological problem regards rather the attempt of post Walrasians to explain historical processes by means of a-historical categories.

Such a method implies that power relations have always existed, even before the historical development of market relations and economic competition. However, they were invisible and could not be detected by scientific investigation. They became visible only with the historical development of capitalism and the consequent possibility of conceiving of a model of complete markets and perfect competition (and, by symmetry, models with imperfections). Post Walrasians must then consider themselves to be very lucky to live in the sole epoch in which everlasting power relations have finally become visible, as an exception to the Walrasian model.

The historical truth, however, is different. Market interaction and economic competition are not at all everlasting forms of social coordination. Markets played only minor roles in pre-capitalist societies and economic competition has become the main form of social coordination only in relatively recent times. If pre-capitalist systems, with less developed or completely absent markets, were not regulated by economic competition, it was not because of *market imperfections* – as post Walrasian economics suggests – but because of *lack of markets*.

Opportunism

Opportunism is the rationality principle of post Walrasian economics. Methodologically, it is a generalisation of Walrasian maximising rationality in a DMC characterised by imperfections. The novelty is only that, in a DMC in which contracts can be violated, optimal strategies might consist in promising one thing and doing another. Optimisation and opportunism are therefore the same thing in this DMC. In a sense, the introduction of opportunism is itself a consequence of the introduction of imperfections.

As a methodological byproduct of Walrasian categories, opportunism is introduced without explanations. The rise of opportunistic behaviours is assumed to be a natural fact, a consequence of human nature. For some reasons (which I will discuss later), post Walrasians are more attracted by workers' opportunism than by capitalists' one. Even workers' opportunism, however, is mainly seen as an everlasting problem stemming from the very nature of the worker, not as a historical product of this mode of production.

In his discussion of the working day, Marx (1867, ch. 10) points out that the establishment of a 'normal working day' was the product of centuries of class struggle. During this process, it was not possible to conceive of workers' behaviour as 'cheating', since there was yet no social standard of what a normal worker should do. It is only when institutional disciplinary apparatuses emerged (with all the consequences studied by Michel Foucault) that workers might be divided into 'normal' and 'deviant' and that those more reluctant to accept the discipline of the capitalist mode of production could appear as 'cheaters', to use the terminology of neoclassical economics, or, following Foucault (1977), might even be depicted as 'mad'.

At the same time, Marx describes the growth of opportunism on the capitalists' side: for instance, after the promulgation of the factory acts of the 1840s in Britain, which fixed the length of the working day, a great deal of cheating was on the side of employers, who just altered the factory clock in order to get extra labour-time.

Although post Walrasians conceive of opportunism as a natural starting point and a universal explanatory cause, it is in fact a product of complex historical processes that have transformed labour into alienated labour and the owners of the means of production into capitalists. These are the preconditions for a problem of monitoring and disciplining labour to emerge. The a-historical methodology of post Walrasian economics does not allow grasping the historical nature of the problem it tries to rationalise. Rather, it suggests that disciplining labour is a universal problem and that its explanatory causes must be a-historical categories. Historically, however, both the problem and its causes are products of this mode of production.

Power and competition

A methodological apparatus based on a-historical categories leads inevitably to other a-historical categories. Power in this conception exists only as a violation of perfect competition. It coexists with competition because, in imperfect DMCs, it is more efficient to have two coordinating mechanisms rather than one. But both power and competition exist out of history, as abstract forms of interpersonal relationships.

Post Walrasian economics does not even try to explain the real processes through which authority and coercive mechanisms have developed in capitalism and have transformed competition into a coercive force. On the contrary, it defines power in such a way that it be incompatible with competition. Competition is so emptied of its coercive nature and the forms of coercion existing in capitalism are sought out of it. The power-free nature of competition is not a result of the analysis, but a definition. If Walras provided an apparent scientific support to the myth of competition as a natural and socially beneficial mechanism, post Walrasian authors willy-nilly support a new myth: the idea that competition is the reign of freedom, in which there is no room for power and coercion.

Here however we have another ideological intrusion hidden behind apparently methodological choices. Methodologically, the problem of this conception of power and competition as abstract, mutually incompatible, categories implies that this framework cannot explain both of them. It must assume one in order to characterise the other as its violation. Competition and power are therefore perfectly symmetrical in this methodology. So, why do post Walrasian economists treat them asymmetrically?

As we have seen, without exceptions, post Walrasians take power as the phenomenon to explain and competition as a natural and everlasting category, deserving no scientific explanation. 'In the beginning there were markets' is Williamson's explicit starting point. Not of course real markets, but neoclassical markets, with atomistic agents and perfect competition. By contrast, power is seen as an unnatural phenomenon simply because it does not exist in Walras' model. This is the origin of the problem.

The idea that competition is a natural mode of interaction between isolated individuals pursuing their private interests has been severely criticised by Marx. As he says, with a highly developed division of labour, 'private interest is already a socially determined interest, which can be achieved only within the conditions laid down by society and with the means provided by society' (Marx 1857, notebook 1, chapter on Money). Competition, therefore, is not merely a mechanism whereby isolated individuals pursue their autonomous goals, according to their innate preferences, but a mode of coordination of social individuals, with convergent and divergent social interests, influenced largely by class relations. Competition cannot precede social interaction, but necessarily follows it.

Before explaining power as a violation of perfect competition, post Walrasians should explain why they choose precisely competition as their starting point. If they do not even raise the question, it is only because the starting point is itself a product of bourgeois ideology: in capitalism, competition appears as natural and Walras' model only formalises this appearance.

As-if economic history

In the debate on power, the application of a static method to explain historical processes has been discussed accurately by Williamson (1975, 1980, 1985, 1996A). Let us follow the mode of reasoning of the Nobel laureate. With his market-hierarchy's framework, he interprets the institutions of capitalism as the product of an evolutionary process towards economic optimality started from a hypothetical perfectly competitive OS. His argument however is purely speculative. He does not investigate what has effectively taken place in history, but analyses the conditions that make institutional arrangements efficient and from this deduces their historical emergence.

Remember that 'in the beginning there were markets' is introduced as a narrative expedient in a context of comparative statics, in which this assumption is not restrictive. Soon after the construction of his market-hierarchy's framework, however, Williamson uses it to explain a number of historical processes and to engage in the historical debate on the origin of hierarchies. His arguments address the work of Sidney Pollard (1965), for example, who stress the need for hierarchical management and control in the light of technological developments and the factory system. Specifically, Williamson criticises the work of the radical political economist Marglin (1974) and argues that power-oriented explanations of firm-hierarchy have weak explanatory power. Against these theories, he argues that wage-labour, firm-hierarchies and all the institutions of capitalism were voluntarily selected for efficiency reasons, without any form of coercion.[1]

But since his arguments are conducted deductively rather than historically, Williamson is forced to *invent* a course of history whose realism and grounding in historical events is immaterial to the validity of the model. 'Predictive power', rather than historical accuracy, seems to drive the argument (cf. Friedman 1953). As a method of history this comes close to being absurd since the validity of our knowledge of the past cannot, by definition, be its predictive power. The only way out of this dilemma for Williamson is to assume that the same operative mechanisms have been ubiquitous throughout history. This however leads to serious tensions in his historical account.

Effectively disregarding serious historical research, Williamson is forced to tell a story that simply fits his theory. He does not try to explain actual events, but only illustrates, *at best* (but probably not!), a *possible* historical development. The story does not start with 'once upon a time...', but with 'let us assume that the world is *as if* it were coherent with our theory...'. In Williamson's theory, as in post Walrasian economics at large, history is treated as if it did not matter to the conception of the model; rather history is 'as-if' to the validity of the model (Ankarloo 2002). But, since hierarchical organisations of production in history preceded a system of markets, feudalism preceded capitalism, the labour market, proletarisation, etc. are historical products, the assumptions of Williamson's theory inevitably land him in trouble.

In order to solve the problem, Williamson depicts micro-economically-rational agents *selecting, voluntarily through conscious choice,* markets over hierarchy, capitalism over feudalism, wage-labour over serfdom, by calculating their respective efficiency.[2] But there is a tension in this account of both rational choice and selection arguments of efficiency. If markets are assumed to exist *prior* to selection, nobody could have historically chosen them for their efficiency (i.e. the market cannot be explained from an efficiency point of view). Alternatively, if markets are seen as consciously chosen, markets cannot be seen as the unintended, 'spontaneous' result of evolution, of a societal 'natural selection'.

Williamson is caught in the middle. The first argument maintains bounded rationality, and efficiency is guaranteed through selection. Faced with the criticism that this argument is theoretically unsound and historically false, Williamson recurs to a second argument, the omnipotent rational economic man, who chooses the best institutional system. And when this is duly criticised for its implicit Panglossianism (Granovetter 1985, Hodgson 1988, 1991, 1994), he comes up again with bounded rationality and selection (Williamson 1996A).

Williamson tries to solve these dilemmas by escaping from them. Markets are everywhere. Capitalist micro-rationality is a universal trait of human beings (even in the absence of prices and markets). But his assumptions are not historically founded and true only for the capitalist system. They remain inadequate for explanations of other systems and for the explanation of the transition to capitalism. Hence, in post Walrasian economics, the problem of how to explain the transition to capitalism is not *solved* but *dissolved*. But granted the fact that capitalism – including capitalist markets and firms – is a result of history, the market too should be considered as a consequence, not the cause of historical development.

History and efficiency

The attempt to interpret actual phenomena as products of hypothetical historical processes is a general feature of post Walrasian economics. This method, however, creates more problems than it solves. First, as we have seen, theoretically, there is no reason why a system should evolve towards Pareto optimality. This might be the case if an existing Pareto optimal equilibrium is also stable and unique, but not otherwise. More generally, this equation evolution-efficiency has been convincingly criticised by institutionalist scholars, who reject the neoclassical foundations of the new institutionalist project (Hodgson 1994).

Second, methodologically, this functionalist mode of explanation presupposes that existing rules and institutions are necessarily optimal (otherwise they would not exist) and that the *status quo* is the best of all possible worlds. This engenders an ambiguity in the normative or positive content of the theory. At first sight, the objective of the theory seems to be merely normative: the problem is not to understand the historical development of capitalist institutions, but rather to specify the conditions under which different modes of interaction efficiently solve predefined economic problems. Thereafter, however, post Walrasian theorists use their normative framework to explain reality as well, and assume that *if it is efficient, it is likely to be observed empirically.*

With respect to economic historians, they thus go the other way round. They do not start from the past in order to *explain* the present; rather, they start from the present and *assume* that the past was such that the present is economically superior to it.

This curious historical method makes the understanding of real capitalism problematic. It is only by starting from the inspection of real pre-capitalist systems that we can understand the historical origin of real capitalist economies. If, on the contrary, we start our evolutionary theory by assuming an imaginary system we cannot but end up with the theoretical understanding of an imaginary world. If we want to understand reality, the hypotheses must be founded in reality. Otherwise we understand a system which is purely ideal and that has no relation with real capitalism.

Whatever may be the engine of institutional change, we would expect present institutional arrangements to be the product of the evolution of preceding arrangements. But if we assume a primordial *ideal* system that has never existed, we prevent ourselves from understanding the *real*, actual system. Only if the historical facts that preceded the advent of capitalism were totally irrelevant for the establishment of capitalist institutions, would the choice of the primordial institutional context not be a problem for the analysis of capitalist institutions.

And, even though in non-capitalist societies markets do not exist or, at best, play a very subordinate role in economic life, in post Walrasian economics, they are ubiquitous. Instead of attempting to understand actual society as a result of the evolution of preceding societies, post Walrasian economics pretends to understand the past as if it had worked according to the same principles as the present. Post Walrasians tell a story of capitalism as if its mechanisms and principles were always present. But, as this is not true, they are obliged to move away from history and to invent a (false) story whose point of arrival is the actual institutional system. The hypothesis that markets have always existed is then inevitable. The method of explaining capitalist institutions is based on the construction of a story, which fits the theory. The goal is to *define* reality in accordance with theory, not to provide a theory that explains reality.

Free contracting, imperfections and class relations

Before capitalism, in this conception, there was not feudalism, or other modes of production, but Léon Walras. The nature of power relations is not studied as a transformation of the power relations that regulated the modes of production that preceded capitalism. Rather, it is explained as a deviation of real capitalism from the abstract Walras' model.

According to Walras and post Walrasians, a world of perfect information and free contracting is, by definition, a world free from power relations. This is why, theoretically, post Walrasian economics needs imperfections to deal with power-related phenomena. The fact that contracting agents might face completely different material constraints when they 'freely' sign the contract is not seen as a potential cause of their power relation. Their different role in production as members of opposing social classes plays no role in the explanation of their power relationship. On the contrary, the implicit assumption is that contracts are signed in a vacuum in which only subjective choice matters.

As Marx (1867, ch. 6) has shown, however, free contracting is only one of the historical conditions of the emergence of proper capitalistic relations. But, for a capitalist-worker relation to emerge, the labourer must be free in a double sense: 'That as a free man, he can dispose of his labour-power as his own commodity, and that on the other hand he has no other commodity for sale, is short of everything necessary for the realisation of his labour-power'.

Free contracting and the lack of the means of production are the two ingredients of capitalistic exploitation. There is no abuse, no asymmetric information or bounded rationality, in the power relation of the capitalist over the worker. The fact that the latter obeys the former is not even the essence of the problem in Marx's ontology. Their interpersonal power relation depends on the relation of exploitation existing between their social classes. Therefore, the coercive nature of capitalism is not sought in the single interpersonal relation between a capitalist and a worker in isolation, but in the social mechanisms that separate the population in social classes and that reproduce this social structure.

In this ontology – built explicitly on the conditions of reproduction of the capitalist mode of production – individual freedom in exchange and social coercion in production are part of the same mode of exploitation. Alchian and Demsetz are then right when they affirm that the worker is a free individual, who can leave the capitalist whenever he/she wants. But this is only one side of the coin. Capitalism would not reproduce itself just by means of exchanges between grocers and customers. Only, in the abstract reign of free contracts, this relation is formally equivalent to the capitalist-worker one. In real capitalism, the coin has a second side. The worker is still free to interrupt the relation with the capitalist, but his/her freedom of choice is very peculiar: he/she *must* obey a capitalist or *choose* another capitalist to obey (or more realistically, hope *to be chosen* by a capitalist). And the worst thing that can happen to a worker, in a society based on capital, is not to enter in relation with any capitalist wishing to command and exploit him/her.

It is not a problem of uncertainty, bounded rationality or asymmetric information: the worker may know or ignore that, within capitalist firms, he/she must obey the capitalist and give him part of the value he/she produces; but, these are the rules of the game and if he/she does not accept them, he/she will not get the means of subsistence. This is not to say that imperfections are useless categories. On the contrary, if one introduces them explicitly in this more accurate ontology, it is evident that asymmetric information, bounded rationality and other 'imperfections' modify the existing power relations. But they do not create them: if a worker is not well informed or is rationally bounded, he/she might accept worse conditions than his/her colleagues. Yet, even the most rational and well informed worker will never get a job if he/she is not ready to obey and to be exploited.

By contrast, post Walrasian economics introduces imperfections in a contradictory ontology, in which capitalism is reduced to free contracting. In Walras' model, this assumption is coupled with the perfect DMC. The result is a conception in which, by assumption, the only coordinating mechanism is competition. In the ontology of post Walrasian economics, free contracting is analysed instead within an imperfect DMC. The result is a conception in which power relations exist, beside competition, but, by construction, only as a consequence of imperfections.

This suggests a picture of a society in which contracts are the highest expression of individual freedom and power relations emerge only when their enforcement is problematic. Bowles and Gintis criticised the Walrasian model on the ground that it deals with these problems by simply assuming that *a handshake is a handshake* – if you make a deal, you have to respect it. In their post Walrasian world, however, things are not so different: a handshake by an opportunist person is no longer a valid handshake, but, exactly like in the Walrasian world, *a contract is a contract* – if you sign it, it is because you want to.

In this conception, power and coercion can arise only when contracts are violated. Marx's critique is so dismissed, without even considering it: in the search of the forms of coercion of this mode of production, Marx's theoretical concern is not the contracts are sometimes violated, but they are generally respected.

Exchange without production

The assumption of pre-existing markets in the analysis of capitalism is as old as the history of political economy. Not much younger is the tradition of criticism of such an assumption initiated by Marx and Engels. The latter notes: 'Production may occur without exchange, but exchange – by the very fact that it is only an exchange of products – cannot occur without production' (Engels 1877, p. 186).

In the debate on power, this distinction between exchange and production is addressed by Frederick Fourie (1989, 1991, 1993). He too argues that exchange presupposes production. So, logically, the firm precedes the market, not vice versa. Otherwise there would be nothing to exchange. Fourie (1993, p. 44) says:

> Firms can exist without markets, i.e. without barter or trade. However, a market, unlike a firm, cannot produce. Therefore market relations can only *link* firms (producing units). ... Markets and firms are not alternative modes of production, but are inherently and essentially dissimilar. ... Therefore, although some firms may in practice be formed or adapted in order to eliminate or avoid market (exchange) transactions, *the emergence and existence of the firm as such – of all firms – cannot be explained by transaction cost considerations*.

Therefore, the idea that the market is an original institution is inconsistent: markets cannot exist without institutions that solve the production problem.[3] So, at the very starting point of the parallel debates on the nature of the firm and the origins of power, one major aspect of the firm is conspicuously absent: the fact that the firm is a *production unit* (Fourie 1989, 1993, Sawyer 1993, Dietrich 1994, Khalil 1995). Even in the absence of imperfections, there would still have to be some *production* unit which is not a market – e.g., family, clan or firm – eventually working on the basis of power relations. To analytically separate the market and the firm, first of all the *firm* must be seen as a production *organisation*.

The attempt to explain the firm as a substitute for the market is ontologically meaningless. One is a productive organisation, the other an exchange institution. Rather than explaining an organisation in light of an institution, one should explain an organisation in light of other organisations. The capitalist firm does not substitute the market but other alternative hierarchical production units (the manor system, family production, the putting out system, etc.).

In post Walrasian economics instead all economic institutions are constructed to solve the same problem: *the allocation of scarce resources*. There is *the one* economic problem and a number of instruments – alternative economic institutions – to solve it. The necessity to resort to different instruments depends on the assumption of a complex DMC in which each of them may fail. The relation among the institutions of capitalism is thus one of pure *substitution*: the space reserved for one institution cannot help but be taken over by other institutions. In this ontology, the coexistence of markets and firms is a problem of *balance* among different instruments. Were we to assume away the reasons for their failures, a single-institution-system would become perfectly consistent.

If, however, we recognise that the allocation function cannot be performed if other functions are not taken care of, the idea itself of a single-institution-system is problematic. In this case it is necessary to assume the existence of production units, without which there would be nothing to exchange. Although these organisations might perform also exchange functions and overlap to some extent with other exchange institutions, their relation with the market cannot be one of pure substitution. Rather productive organisations and markets are necessary complements to one another in capitalism. In Marx's words:

> Production by an isolated individual outside society [...] is as much of an absurdity as is the development of language without individuals living *together* and talking to each other. There is no point in dwelling on this any longer. The point could go entirely unmentioned if this twaddle, which had sense and reason for the eighteenth-century characters, had not been earnestly pulled back into the centre of the most modern economics.
>
> (Marx 1857, Notebook M, Introduction)

Very simply, the conception of a primordial system of pure markets is internally inconsistent, because the working of an exchange institution requires the existence of productive organisations.

Production, circulation and the free trader vulgaris

In Marx's characterisation of capitalism as a system of commodity production, there is a clear-cut separation between the spheres of production and circulation of commodities. This separation allows him discussing how capital may appear to be productive (in circulation), notwithstanding its unproductive nature (in production) and criticising the economic conceptions based solely on circulation.

In the sphere of circulation, capitalists and workers do not appear in the first instance as social entities, but simply as individuals who exchange commodities. As such, they seem to be on the same ground and their relation seems to be based purely on free will: 'There alone rule Freedom, Equality, Property and Bentham', says Marx (1867, ch. 6) provocatively. But before being exchanged, commodities must be produced. Before discussing the forms of power originating directly in the sphere of circulation, Marx explains thus the forms of coercion emanating from production. As he writes:

> On leaving this sphere of simple circulation or of exchange of commodities, which furnishes the 'Free-trader Vulgaris' with his views and ideas, and with the standard by which he judges a society based on capital and wages, we think we can perceive a change in the physiognomy of our dramatis personae. He, who before was the money-owner, now strides in front as capitalist; the possessor of labour-power follows as his labourer. The one with an air of importance, smirking, intent on business; the other, timid and holding back, like one who is bringing his own hide to market and has nothing to expect but – a hiding.
>
> (Marx 1867, ch. 6)

By investigating the sphere of production, Marx argued that the working class is exploited and that the capitalist class appropriates a value it has not produced. This form of social exploitation is also the main cause of the asymmetry between capitalists and workers in the workplace. Historically, the need to control and supervise the production process is a consequence of the problematic process of extracting living labour from workers' labour power. Marx discusses this process in different parts of *Capital* and explains how the internal organisation of the firm and the way workers are disciplined in the workplace evolve according to the needs of capital accumulation. He points out for instance that the development of stock companies and cooperative factories are very different processes, but are also responses to the same problem: in one case, the extraction of living labour from workers' labour power is delegated to a manager, in the other to workers themselves (Marx 1894, ch. 27).

Modern Marxists, such as Harry Braverman (1974), Marglin (1974, 1975, 1991), and Edwards (1979) have developed this conception by discussing the evolution of class relationships and the development of different forms of power, authority and hierarchy within capitalist firms in the twentieth century. Social exploitation and interpersonal power relations, in the work of these authors, are dialectically linked: on the one hand, exploitative class relations in society are the cause of the interpersonal power relation in the workplace; on the other hand, the evolution of the forms of power prevailing within capitalist firms transforms class relations and modifies the rate of exploitation.

In this ontology, the forms of power that prevail in the sphere of production are linked to the exchanges that must occur in circulation in order for the system to reproduce itself. Capitalist production starts with the sale of workers' labour power. By buying this commodity, the capitalist acquires the right to dispose of it. It is not a question of price. The worker might sell it dear or cheap, but the very act of selling his/her labour power confers the capitalist an interpersonal power over him/her during the production process.

The post Walrasian approach to power however does not start from the real development of capitalism and its reproducing mechanisms, but from an abstract model, based on a flat ontology in which production is, *de facto*, a sub-set of circulation, an exchange between input owners. The result is a more sophisticated ontology, still based on pure circulation, in which however circulation incorporates imperfections. Even the central relation that characterises production – the capitalist-worker relationship – is considered as a form of exchange, an exchange that occurs in a complex DMC, but still a phenomenon of circulation.

Within the sphere of circulation, there can be no production of value but only an exchange of equivalents. Therefore, if, in an equilibrium position, the individual capitalist has power over the individual worker, it is only because he pays for it. Before the exchange, the information advantage belonged to the worker, like the labour power that he/she sells to the capitalist. After the exchange, power is in the hands of the capitalist, and its monetary equivalent in the pockets of the worker.

In this ontology, the price that the capitalist pays to have power over the worker is not simply the wage, as Marx argued, but a part of it. In post Walrasian economics, by definition, market clearing wages involve no power relations. The latter arise only when the capitalist pays additional money to induce worker's self-discipline. Power is thus a sort of commodity, which the capitalist buys from the worker – besides his/her labour power – in order to increase his/her productivity, exactly as he buys machines, work instruments and innovative technologies. Like all commodities, power has its equilibrium price, defined as the amount of money that compensates the worker for not using his/her informative advantages opportunistically.

As Marx has explained, independent on the real origin of value, to the eyes of the capitalist, the value of production is produced by the total capital he has invested. By formally including power in the reign of commodities, neoclassical radicals preserve this appearance. If the capitalist buys a machine or a power relation, it is only because the increase in expected revenues is greater than the cost of the investment. For him, power relations are production factors, no less than any other work instrument he buys in order to increase workers' productivity. Therefore, the increase in the value of production following the purchase of a power relation over the worker appears to him as an effect of the capital spent in this investment, not as a consequence of the increase in worker's effort (which, in Marxist terms, corresponds to an increase in the amount of living labour extracted by his/her labour power).

Without any ontological separation between production and circulation, the appearances that capital is productive and that individuals are equal becomes in post Walrasian economics the true essence of capitalism. In this mystified conception, the asymmetry responsible for eventual power relations must be introduced directly in circulation, even when dealing with capitalists and workers. Formal equality in the market becomes synonymous of 'freedom' and power relations are detected only when they manifest themselves formally in asymmetric market relations. All other forms of coercion of capitalism become invisible.

But, even within this narrow conception based on circulation, post Walrasian economics fails to develop a general theory of power. Contrary to the claim of radical economists, power can only be an exception in this approach, but cannot be the rule. If all workers were really difficult to monitor and endowed with information advantages because of widespread imperfections in the DMC, no competitive wage in the market would exist. Therefore, the threat of being fired and losing the employment rent would not be credible, and the capitalist would have no power over them. Remember that in this theory of power, just as in the efficiency wages theory, the worker has an incentive to work hard only if a lower (perfectly competitive) wage prevails in the labour market. In other words, this theory can, at best, explain why some particular workers suffer a power relation from their employer, but it cannot explain why workers in general suffer a power relation from capitalists. On the contrary, the demonstration that some individual workers suffer a power relation rests on the assumption that standard workers suffer none.

Scientific research and cultural hegemony

Before closing my critical revisitation of the post Walrasian approach to power, let me discuss the ideological nature of the scientific problem developed in the debate. As we have seen, post Walrasian economics inherits the assumption of self-interested individuals from Walrasian economics. However, it describes self-interested behaviour as 'profit maximisation' with regard to the capitalist and as 'opportunism', 'shirking' or 'cheating' with regard to the worker. The problem is not only terminological. It reflects rather a precise, although implicit, ideological position.

Contemporary capitalism offers a wide range of examples of contracts that are not enforced correctly: workers that are not paid for months by their employers, banks that do not pay back depositors' money, states that do not honour their international commitments, women that are molested in the workplace. These are not distortions of capitalism, but normal effects of self-interested behaviours in a society characterised by asymmetrical power relations.

With asymmetric power relations, it is clear that the powerful, not the powerless, can more easily behave opportunistically. For some reason, however, when the capitalist-worker relationship is at stake, post Walrasians are preoccupied mainly by the possibility that the worker takes a break, slows down the pace of work or does not maximise his/her effort during the working day – problems that perhaps should concern more the capitalist than the economist. This is the origin of the literature on monitoring, shirking, incentive schemes, principal-agent problems and the rest.

As we have seen, the post Walrasian framework has been applied to very different situations in which contract enforcement is problematic. Curiously, however, no post Walrasian focuses on the millions of workers that suffer daily abuses of their boss, but have no means (and perhaps no interest) to bring him to the tribunal; or on those who just accept the contract because they have no alternative, no matter the terms of the contract; or on those masses of illegal migrant workers who cannot even aspire to get a contract, but work harder than the others, without any right, under the unappealable direction of a racist boss. By assumption, as Bowles and Gintis say explicitly, the employer's promises are legally enforceable and the problem is only on the worker's side.

Formally, there is no asymmetry between capitalists and workers in this theoretical framework. As self-interested individuals, they will contravene their commitments every time this increases their expected utility. In concrete model building, however, post Walrasians treat these two figures asymmetrically: one is the supervisor, the other the supervised, one is the principal, the other the agent; and the 'scientific problem' is to find effective disciplining and supervising methods that push the agent to serve at best the interests of the principal. Implicitly or explicitly, capitalists' interests are transformed into social goals.

Starting from a symmetrical conflict, post Walrasians introduce an asymmetry and put themselves at the service of one of the conflicting parties. There is no theoretical reason why the economist should take the viewpoint of the capitalist, rather than that of the worker. But once this theoretical choice has been taken, implicitly or explicitly, all issues of 'cheating', 'shirking' and 'laziness' follow naturally. This is why, in this literature, the lazy one is the worker, who works 7 hours and 55 minutes (having 'shirked' 5 minutes in the toilets), not the capitalist who does not work at all.

Theoretically, there is no obstacle that prevents neoclassical economists from developing also the social consequences of capitalists' opportunistic strategies against their employees. If this occurs rarely it is because the scientific community has its own internal logic. As Antonio Gramsci (1929–35) has pointed out in his study of cultural hegemony and the role of intellectuals, dominant ideology tends to impose the viewpoint of the ruling class as a cultural norm.

Post Walrasian economics is both a cause and an effect in this process. On the one hand, its scientific problem is a product of capitalist ideology: the problem is to monitor and discipline labour. On the other hand, by transforming the capitalist's problem (worker's opportunism) into a social problem, it reinforces the idea that workers' discipline is a universal goal and that all studies developing explicitly the standpoint and the interests of the worker are politically biased, hence, according to the dominant conception, not really scientific.

Before Marxists converted to neoclassical methodology (and neoliberal ideology) took this route, the scientific defence of capitalists' interests in the workplace was not hidden behind questions of Pareto optimality and second-best solutions. Both Marxists and bourgeois economists agreed that a greater effort at work was in the interest of capitalists and went against those of the working class.

When in 1911 Frederick Taylor wrote *The principles of scientific management* – in which he studied how to increase workers' productivity and how to extract as much labour as possible from their labour power – its impact in the political and scientific debate was unambiguous: his work was appreciated not only by capitalists – which is quite obvious – but also by mainstream economists. Rapidly, scientific management affirmed itself as a new research program, with new university teachings and specialised academic journals. In the Marxist camp, this managerial approach was openly criticised, both theoretically and politically, with the development of the so called *labour process debate*.

Taylor of course was not a Marxist and was perfectly aware that his fortune was due to his ability to put science at the service of the capitalist class. Less evident, by contrast, are the real intentions of radicals, who accept neoclassical economics as a matter of pure methodology, without understanding the underlying ontology and without discussing the relations between ideology and methodology. Because the concrete effect of their theories is straightforward: in a historical context, in which the labour movement was trying to unite and organise in the workplace and in the overall society, post Walrasians have contributed to rationalise the everlasting problem of the capitalist class – to discipline labour and organise it according to capital needs – and to reinforce a conception in which power is only an interpersonal affair.

Conclusions

Let me recap my arguments by going backward, from the pre-scientific choices of post Walrasian economics, to methodology and ontology. In the analysis of the capitalist-worker relationship, post Walrasians – from ultra-liberals to radicals – have unanimously focused on the capitalist's standpoint and have thus contributed to rationalise and solve his economic problem. In this way – in some cases, doubtless, involuntarily – they have transformed a problem of a part of society into a problem of the entire society. This choice involves a stronger role for ideology than in Walrasian economics. The latter only attempts to formalise the virtues of market interactions among atomised individuals. Post Walrasian economics goes further. Within the same individualist framework, which assigns no role to class relations, it introduces social classes surreptitiously by defining 'the economic problem' as 'the problem of the capitalist'. This ideological degeneration of radical thinking – I suggest – is the outcome of two interdependent processes: 1) the tendency to a-critically accept neoclassical methodology in the scientific community; 2) the consolidation of the neoliberal hegemony in culture and society.

Post Walrasian methodology is based on two main ingredients: imperfections and opportunism. These ingredients are defined a-historically. The resulting conception of power is a-historical as well. The different forms that power takes in the history of capitalism are not objects of scientific inquiry. The goal is rather to show that is a valid alternative to competition, under certain conditions. The result is a theory of power in which, by construction, competition is power-free. In post Walrasian economics, the coercive law of capitalism is not competition, as Marx thought, but the lack of it.

These a-historical categories are developed within a comparative statics framework, as possible explanations of real historical processes, by choosing convenient hypothetical initial conditions. This method does not even try to *explain* the present as the result of the processes of the past; instead, it *assumes* the past in order to make the present appear Pareto superior. Economic historians, in their attempt to explain the course of history, provide a picture of the present made up of contradictions, conflicts, convergences and divergences. Williamson and post Walrasian economics, instead assume that the present is a coherent expression of rationality and efficiency and invent a story whose logical end is the existing reality indeed. So, what for the historians are contradictions and compromises become for post Walrasians the conditions of consistency. This implies that the stories told by economic historians and by post Walrasians go in opposite directions: from the past to the present in the first case, from the present to the past in the second. Economic historians try to explain history, post Walrasian economists, instead, tells a fairy-tale whose happy ending is the present. If David Hume urged that it is not scientifically correct to deduce *what ought to be* from *what is*, here we have *what is* being deduced from *what ought to be*, which is no less methodologically unsound.

This methodology imposes new conditions on the implicit ontology of Walras' model. In post Walrasian economics, capitalists and workers are not social entities, developing in a particular historical context, but individuals with everlasting innate qualities. Their eventual power relation depends only on these qualities and on their fit with an imperfect DMC. The fact that one is a capitalist and the other a worker is irrelevant. They might also be a bank and a firm, two states, or a customer and a grocer. As long as the parameters of the models coincide, the nature of the power relation is the same. And as power arises in circulation, where only exchanges of equivalents occur, the interpersonal asymmetry before the exchange must be assumed to be favourable to the worker if one wants to prove that, after the exchange – when individual advantages have been monetised – power is in the hands of the capitalist.

When we move from the formal demonstration that the capitalist has power over the worker to a discussion of the causes and the mechanisms of this power relation, the result is not so Marxist. Rather, it is a logical development of the mystified conception formalised by Walras. The proof is that, in these models, power is a form of capital and, as such, is treated as productive. But this also confirms that post Walrasian economics is only a sophisticated version of the old bourgeois conception criticised by Marx, in which all forms of capital are conceptualised as productive. My conclusion is that, overall, post Walrasian economics is a coherent extension of perfect exchange to contested exchange. The obvious consequence, however, is the addition of new contradictions to an already contradictory conception.

To explain how even Marx-sympathisers in this approach converge on the same conception of power of ultra-liberal anti-Marxists we must now turn our attention to competition. The similarities in their conceptions of power are in fact a consequence of their common mystified conception of competition. The problem is thus to explain how this mystified conception has become the starting point of a whole generation of academicians and, more generally, how competition has affirmed itself in society as a natural mode of interaction and a universal political guide. Only after an organic critique of competition can we come back to power and complete the discussion of the ideological and political role of post Walrasian economics in scientific research and in class struggle.

Notes

1 This assumption is developed also by another Nobel Prize, Stiglitz (1975), and is shared by post Walrasian economics at large, spanning from Cheung (1983) to Putterman (1995), a contractualist and a radical respectively. However, historians of labour relations and firm-hierarchies – whether Marxist (Thompson 1978, 1993, Hobsbawn 1964, Rule 1986), or power oriented (Marglin 1974, 1975, 1991), or technology oriented (Landes 1969, Berg 1984, 1991, Pollard 1965), or even influenced by post-structuralist deconstruction (Berlanstein 1993) – all seem to converge on the point that capitalist hierarchies were imposed on workers and entrepreneurs alike, with ample resistance from workers and independent producers and without any of the 'voluntary exchanges' depicted in the fairytales of post Walrasian economics.

2 This is also the general method developed by North in his new institutional approach to economic history (North and Thomas 1973, North 1981).

3 Even North (1981, p. 41) points out: 'All the modern neoclassical literature discusses the firm as a substitute for the market. [This] ignores a crucial fact of history: hierarchical organization forms and contractual arrangements in exchange predate the price making market'.

References

Ankarloo, Daniel (2002), New institutional economics and economic history, *Capital and Class*, vol. 78, pp. 9–36.

Berg, Maxine (1984), *The age of manufactures*, London, Fontana.

——(1991), On the origins of capitalist hierarchy, in Gustavsson, Bo (ed.), *Power and economic institutions*, Aldershot, Edward Elgar.

Berlanstein, Lenard (1993), *Rethinking labor history: Essays on discourse and class analysis*, Urbana, University of Illinois Press.

Braverman, Harry (1974), *Labour and monopoly capital: The degradation of work in the twentieth century*, New York, Monthly Review Press.

Cheung, Stephen (1983), The contractual nature of the firm, *Journal of Law and Economics*, vol. 26, n. 1, pp. 1–21.

Dietrich, Michael (1994), *Transaction cost economics and beyond*, London, Routledge.

Edwards, Richard (1979), *Contested terrain: The transformation of the workplace in the twentieth century*, New York, Basis Books.

Engels, Frederick (1877), *Anti-Dühring. Herr Eugen Dühring's revolution in science*. Retrieved from www.marxists.org/archive/marx/works/1877/anti-duhring (accessed 1 March 2016).

Foucault, Michel (1977), *Discipline and punish: The birth of the prison*, London, Allen Lane.

Fourie, Frederick (1989), The nature of firms and markets: Do transaction cost theories help?, *The South African Journal of Economics*, vol. 57, n. 2, pp. 142–60.

——(1991), The nature of the market: A structural analysis, in Hodgson, Geoffrey and Ernesto Screpanti (eds), *Rethinking economics: Markets, technology and economic evolution*, Aldershot, Edward Elgar.

——(1993), In the beginning there were markets?, in Pitelis, Christos (ed.), *Transaction costs, markets and hierarchies*, Oxford, Basil Blackwell.

Friedman, Milton (1953), The methodology of positive economics, in Friedman, Milton (ed.) *Essays in positive economics*, Chicago, University of Chicago Press.

Gramsci, Antonio (1929–35), *Prison notebooks*. Retrieved from www.marxists.org/archive/gramsci/prison_notebooks/index.htm (accessed 1 March 2016).

Granovetter, Mark (1985), Economic action and social structure: The problem of embeddedness, *Journal of American Sociology*, vol. 91, n. 3, pp. 481–510.

Hobsbawn, Eric (1964), *Labouring men: Studies in the history of labor*, London, Weidenfield and Nicolson.

Hodgson, Geoffrey (1988), *Economics and institutions*, Cambridge, Polity Press.

——(1991), Economic evolution, intervention contra Pangloss, *Journal of Economic Issues*, vol. 25, n. 2, pp. 519–33.

——(1994), Evolution and optimality, in Hodgson, Geoffrey, Warren Samuels and Marc Tool (eds), *The Elgar companion to institutional and evolutionary economics*, Aldershot, Edward Elgar.

Khalil, Elias (1995), Organization versus institutions, *Journal of Institutional and Theoretical Economics*, vol. 151, n. 3, pp. 445–66.

Landes, David (1969), *The unbound prometheus*, Cambridge, Cambridge University Press.

Marglin, Stephen (1974), What do bosses do? The origins and functions of hierarchy in capitalist production, Part 1, *Review of Radical Political Economics*, vol. 6, n. 2, pp. 60–112.

——(1975), What do bosses do? The origins and functions of hierarchy in capitalist production, Part 2, *Review of Radical Political Economics*, vol. 7, n. 1, pp. 20–37.

——(1991), Understanding capitalism: Control versus efficiency, in Gustavsson, Bo (ed.), *Power and economic institutions*, Aldershot, Edward Elgar.

Marx, Karl (1844), *Economic and philosophic manuscripts*. Retrieved from www.marxists.org/archive/marx/works/1844/manuscripts/preface.htm (accessed 1 March 2016).

——(1857), *Outlines of the critique of political economy*. Retrieved from www.marxists.org/archive/marx/works/1857/grundrisse/index.htm (accessed 1 March 2016).

——(1867), *Capital: Critique of political economy, vol, 1, The process of capitalist production*. Retrieved from www.marxists.org/archive/marx/works/1867-c1/index.htm (accessed 18 April 2016).

——(1894), *Capital: Critique of political economy, vol, 3, The process of capitalist production as a whole*. Retrieved from www.marxists.org/archive/marx/works/1894-c3/index.htm (accessed 1 March 2016).

North, Douglas (1981), *Structure and change in economic history*, New York, W.W. Norton.

North, Douglas and Robert Paul Thomas (1973), *The rise of the western world*, Cambridge, Cambridge University Press.

Pollard, Sidney (1965), *The genesis of modern management*, London, Edward Arnold.

Putterman, Louis (1995), Markets, hierarchies and information: On a paradox in the economics of organization, *Journal of Economic Behavior and Organization*, vol. 26, pp. 373–90.

Rule, John (1986), *The labouring classes in early industrial England 1750–1850*, London, Longman.

Sawyer, Malcolm (1993), The nature and role of the market, in Pitelis, Christos (ed.), *Transaction costs, markets and hierarchies*, Oxford, Basil Blackwell.

Stiglitz, Joseph (1975), Incentives, risk, and information: Notes towards a theory of hierarchy, *Bell Journal of Economics*, vol. 6, pp. 552–79.

Taylor, Frederick (1911), *The principles of scientific management*, New York, Harper and Brothers.

Thompson, Edward (1978), *The making of the English working class*, London, Penguin.

——(1993), *Customs in common*, London, Penguin.

Williamson, Oliver (1975), *Markets and hierarchies: Analysis and antitrust implications: A study in the economics of internal organization*, New York, Free Press.

——(1985), *The economic institutions of capitalism: Firms, markets, relational contracting*, New York, Free Press.

——(1993), Contested exchange versus the governance of contractual relations, *Journal of Economic Perspectives*, vol. 7, n. 1, pp. 103–8.

——(1994), Visible and invisible governance, *American Economic Review, Papers and Proceedings*, vol. 84, n. 2, pp. 323–6.

——(1995), Hierarchies, markets and power in the economy: An economic perspective, *Industrial and Corporate Change*, vol. 4, n. 1, pp. 21–49.

——(1996A), *The mechanisms of governance*, Oxford, Oxford University Press.

Part II

The ontology of capitalist power and the coercive law of competition

5 Marx's critique of capital and competition

> Everything appears reversed in competition, and thus in the consciousness of its agents ... The vulgar economist does practically no more than translate the singular concepts of the capitalists, who are in the thrall of competition, into a seemingly more theoretical and generalised language, and attempt to substantiate the justice of those conceptions.
>
> (Marx 1894, ch. 13)

Competition is a magic word in economics and politics. Bourgeois economics treats it as a natural mode of human interaction or even the general form of interaction in the whole biological realm. Within this conception, the scientific problem is not to understand how, in capitalism, economic competition becomes a mechanism – or rather *the* mechanism – of social coordination, but to appraise its economic consequences. This economic appraisal is developed by neoclassical economics by means of the model of perfect competition, a model based on unrealistic assumptions and conceptual problems, which however allows demonstrating the virtues of this mode of interaction: its economic efficiency, its ethical justness and its ability to allow individuals express freely their preferences, without any form of coercion or power relation.

In politics, these 'demonstrations' are the scientific foundation of the neoliberal hegemony of the last decades. In the name of competition, international institutions, national governments and capitalists' associations have imposed capital mobility, work flexibility and processes of privatisation, liberalisation and deregulation, whose effect has been worker precariousness, increased exploitation and an acceleration in the process of commodification of society. Today, to go against competition is simply irrational, inefficient and incompatible with individual freedoms and the common good. These are the terms of the political debate in the neoliberal era.

Competition however is all but a natural phenomenon and its eventual social desirability is first of all a matter of class interests. As Engels (1845, ch. 3) argues, 'competition of the workers among themselves is ... the sharpest weapon against the proletariat in the hands of the bourgeoisie'. From a Marxist perspective, therefore, the scientific problem is not to appraise the desirability of competition, but to understand how it works, the role it plays in the reproduction and development of the capitalist mode of production and its effects on class struggle.

Marx discusses competition as a coercive mechanism, which imposes capital logic on social relations and governs the reproduction of the class structure of society. This is why, in his general critique of the capitalist mode of production, he accepts the assumption of unhampered competition. Unlike liberal (and neoliberal) economists, however, he does not identify a world entirely regulated by competition with the 'Eden of the innate rights of man' (Marx 1867, ch. 6), ruled by equal exchange and individual freedom, but shows rather that it is a world of exploitation and social coercion. The free working of competition is not at all the recomposition of class interest and the end of exploitation, but its opposite: the highest expression of class power and the necessary condition for maximising the rate of surplus value. In this perspective, even the attempt to define normative economic criteria to pursue the common good is a contradiction in terms.

Against those critics who think that Marx's critique is dated, I argue that his analysis of the origins and development of competition in the capitalist mode of production provides a general method for understanding even the most recent transformations that have led to the neoliberal hegemony, including the rise of the myth of perfect competition and the academic research on power. By developing a Marxist conception of competition, my aim is not only to develop the explanation of the mechanisms of capitalist coercion but also to counter scientifically the bourgeois conception and the political implications that follow.

I begin by selecting the works in which Marx discusses competition as a social mechanism imposing the 'coercive laws' of capital. Then, I focus on the distinction between total social capital and competition between individual capitals. Against the appearances, Marx shows that the former has an autonomous existence and its own laws of development, which in fact constrain the development of the latter, rather than the other way round. This is why competition between capitals can be properly understood only after having examined the nature of capital as a whole. Next, I examine the origin of competition. Indeed, this relation between capital and competition shows that competition is not a natural and everlasting mode of human interaction but a historical coordinating mechanism developing with the development of capital.

My exposition continues by discussing the role of competition as the enforcer of capital laws and as the mechanism that regulates the process of capital subsumption. Similarly to Smith and the classics, Marx analyses competition as a mechanism that guides individual choices and produces social effects that go beyond the individual will. Smith's (1776, book 4, ch. 2, par. 9) metaphor is famous: '[every individual] is led by an invisible hand to promote an end which was no part of his intention ... By pursuing his own interest he frequently promotes that of the society more effectually than when he really intends to promote it'. Marx however develops the role of the 'invisible hand' as part of his critique of the contradictions of capital accumulation. The result is a conception of competition diametrically opposed to the Smithian one: the invisible hand does not promote social development and economic growth but only enforces the contradictions of capital. Its social effect is not the harmonious recomposition of individual interests but the subjugation of the whole society under the capital rationale.

I terminate my reconstruction of Marx's critique of capital and competition by presenting their very enemy – association – and by discussing the animated debate on the end of competition. Although in my interpretation of Marx, competition is the only essential, necessary, coercive mechanism of the capitalist mode of production, it generally does not operate in isolation. A second mechanism governing class relations is association. Unlike competition, association does not originate from the essential social relations of capitalism, but is the product of intentional and deliberate choices, often taken as reaction against competition. In their concrete development, competition and association tend to produce monopolistic market forms. Cartels and market power however only supersede the competitive market form, but do not stop the working of the competitive mechanism. They do not mark the end of competition but its development at a higher level. As the enforcer of capitalist laws, competition is not abolished by the rise of 'monopoly capitalism' but by the end of capitalism.

Finally, I discuss the rise of the myth of perfect competition and the role played by bourgeois economics. In the process of commodification of society, competition tends to impose itself at a subjective level as well: as the spectrum of social relations governed by competition develops, the latter tends to appear as a natural force, a form of interaction that has always existed, a consequence of human nature. In this context, neoclassical economics only translates these appearances into a mathematical language and furnishes the politician the 'scientific' arguments for further developing the commodification of society: not of course as an explicit defence of class interests, but in the name of the common good.

Competition in Marx's work

In the attempt to develop a Marxian conception of competition, the first challenge is that, in the *Grundrisse*, Marx explains that he intends to treat such a topic as a separate issue after having explained 'capital in general'. The term 'capital in general', however, does not appear in his main work, *Capital*. This issue has been controversial in Marxist scholarship. Some authors maintain that the three volumes of *Capital* deal in fact with 'capital in general' and contain just the aspects of competition that are strictly necessary for such a purpose. According to this interpretation, there is thus no hope to find a systematic analysis of competition in Marx's own work, since in his life he did not even have the time to finish volume 2 and 3 of *Capital*. By contrast, others argue that Marx finally abandoned the notion of 'capital in general' and, when he organised *Capital* in three volumes, he incorporated his analysis of competition mainly in the third volume and partly in the first one (Rosdolsky 1977, Pilling 1980, Heinrich 1989, Moseley 1993, Arthur 2002, 2010).

In *Capital*, the word 'competition' appears for the first time in volume 1, chapter 10, titled 'The working day', in which Marx explains how competition regulates such a crucial aspect of the conflict between capital and labour in the production of surplus value. In chapter 12, however, he soon clarifies that he does not intend to consider here the way in which the laws of capitalist production 'assert themselves as coercive laws of competition, and are brought home to the mind and consciousness of the individual capitalist as the directing motives of his operations' and reaffirms that 'a scientific analysis of competition is not possible, before we have a conception of the inner nature of capital, just as the apparent motions of the heavenly bodies are not intelligible to any but him, who is acquainted with their real motions, motions which are not directly perceptible by the senses'.

It is only in the third volume – after having shown that capital accumulation is the result of increasing exploitation – that Marx discusses the relations between many individual capitals and deals thus more systematically with the effects of competition (Rosdolsky 1977, ch. 2). More precisely, in chapter 10 of volume 3, he explains the role of competition in the equalisation of the rate of profit. He shows that the price of production includes the average profit and coincides basically with Smith's *natural price*, David Ricardo's *price of production* or *cost of production* and Physiocrats' *prix nécessaire*.

However, contrary to his predecessors, who were not able to explain the nature of profit according to the labour theory of value and saw it as an effect of competition, Marx shows that competition is not the cause of profits but only tends to equalise the rates of profit among the different sectors of the economy, through its effects on the prices of production.

Unlike classical political economist, Marx shows also that within each sector, competition tends to impose a unique price, which implies heterogeneous profit rates, if costs of production are heterogeneous (Chattopadhyay 2012).

Finally, in the last part of the book, Marx discusses the 'Illusions created by competition' (ch. 50). He explains that 'competition already presupposes the existence of profit' and criticises the notion that profits and rents might be created in the sphere of circulation. The strength of his critique rests on the fact that he has already explained the nature of surplus value and capitalist exploitation in the first six parts of volume 1, without recurring to competition (apart from the discussion of how competition imposes the law of capitalist production on both capitalists and workers in the determination of the wage and the length of a normal working day).

How Marx construed methodologically the progression of concepts from volumes 1 and 2 to volume 3 – from the inner nature of capital to the relations between many capitals – has been discussed from many different angles.[1] Notice however that this step does not imply that competition enter properly the scene only in volume 3. In fact, its analysis begins in volume 1, as soon as Marx discusses capital accumulation (part VII).

At this stage of the analysis, accumulation is assumed, rather than explained, Marx's goal here being to show its *effects* on the organic composition of capital and the rate of surplus value. Marx is not yet in position to discuss the relationships among the individual capitals that form the total social capital. Methodologically, such a discussion must be preceded by an analysis of the laws of development of total social capital. However, concretely, it is precisely through these relationships among individual capitals that the social capital develops and accumulates. Although named only few times, competition is thus actively in the background already in the last parts of volume 1 dealing with accumulation.

Without an explicit analysis of the relations between many capitals, all that Marx can say in volume 1 of *Capital* (ch. 24) about the cause of capital accumulation is that it is a 'deliberate act' by the capitalist. But a deliberate act occurring under the pressure of competition: 'Competition makes the immanent laws of capitalist production to be felt by each individual capitalist, as external coercive laws. It compels him to keep constantly extending his capital, in order to preserve it, but extend it he cannot, except by means of progressive accumulation'.

Therefore, if we really had to find the actual place marking the entrance of competition in *Capital*, it would not be in the passage from volumes 1 and 2 to volume 3, but within volumes 1 and 2, in the passages from the analysis of capital production and reproduction to the analysis of its accumulation.

Put simply, by assuming capital accumulation, in part VII of volume 1 (and in the parts of volume 2 in which he looks at the same process from the viewpoint of circulation), Marx assumes competition as well. This is not a methodological oversight but the result of a well-defined scientific project. Firstly, he explains the exploitative nature of capitalist production, by looking at capital as a whole and without recurring to competition (first six parts of volume 1). Then, he focuses on capital accumulation. He starts from its general *effects* – the increase of total social capital – which thus finds its logical place in volume 1 (parts VII and VIII). Here, competition is 'assumed' implicitly and temporarily, together with capital accumulation. Finally, Marx analyses the internal *cause* of capital accumulation by shifting methodologically from total social capital to the relations between many capitals. Here, he shows that competition is a coercive mechanism acting on individual capitals, whose general effect is the process of capital accumulation itself.

His analysis of competition in volume 3, therefore, explains and confirms his initial 'assumption' (or rather, the historical phenomenon to explain) that capital tends in fact to accumulate. In this way, *Capital* is not a trilogy but a unified, organic scientific work. As a result, any attempt to enucleate punctually the role of competition in Marx's work should not be pushed too far since a linear and unidirectional causal nexus between his economic categories is hardly compatible with his dialectical method.

Beside this attempt to integrate organically competition in his critique, Marx develops other reflections on competition in more punctual works. As far as the origins of competition are concerned, perhaps the most explicit discussion is developed by Engels in his *Outlines of a critique of political economy*, where he puts it in relation with the development of private property and market relations. The same issue is dealt with by Marx in the *Economic and philosophical manuscripts of 1844*, in which he criticises bourgeois economists for taking for granted private property and all the categories that presuppose it (including competition) and explains them as a consequence of estranged, alienated labour. In the *Unpublished sixth chapter of the first volume of Capital*, Marx focuses on the relation between the development of competition and the process of subsumption of labour under capital. Finally, in *The poverty of philosophy*, by taking inspiration from the work of Pierre-Joseph Proudhon, he develops his most explicit and polemical arguments against the bourgeois conception of competition.

After Marx's death, his conception of competition has been developed in particular within the debate on imperialism. The historical rise of monopolistic market forms has suggested in fact a contraposition between competition and monopoly. Rudolph Hilferding's *Finance capital* and Lenin's *Imperialism* are the main theoretical references to shed light on the different conceptions of competition as a simple market form or rather as the coordinating and coercing mechanism of capitalism.

Total social capital and competition between individual capitals

In his systematic critique of capital, Marx discusses it both as a social unity and as a multitude of individual capitals in competition with one another. In phenomenal reality, he notices, capital appears as a set of autonomous individual capitals and total capital appears simply as their aggregation. The former appears as the real nature of capital and the latter as a conventional entity, without any real autonomy. It is only by means of scientific analysis that we can grasp the essence of the total social capital and its relation with the individual capitals that constitute it.

Marx's choice to analyse total social capital before discussing competition between capitals is not merely a methodological choice or an expositional expedient. It is rather the result of an ontological argument. Total social capital is not an arbitrary, unreal, abstraction. As Geoff Pilling (1980, ch. 3, sec. 6) argues, 'It is a fallacy to think that because abstractions (such as that of capital in general) are formed through the penetration of the appearance of things, deeper into the essence of the phenomena concerned, this renders such abstractions unreal. On the contrary, they have a powerful objective existence precisely because, as abstractions, they embrace the wealth of all the phenomena concerned'.

Total social capital is an essential abstraction, describing a real entity, with an objective existence in the capitalist mode of production. Its existence is a direct consequence of this peculiar class society, in which interpersonal relations are free at an individual level, but constrained by social relations: as individuals, both the worker and the capitalist meet on a purely voluntary basis; as members of different social classes, however, the former must give the latter a part of the value he/she produces. This is why, in capitalism, exploitation is essentially a social relation, not an interpersonal one, and this is why competition cannot be its cause. Exploitation is a relation between the total social capital and the working class, not a relation between an individual capital and a single worker.

In their need to work to access the means of subsistence, workers face capital as a whole (although, of course, they can at best aspire to enter a relation with only a piece of this social whole): if they do not like the particular capitalist who exploit them, they can look for another capitalist willing to exploit them more gently, but they cannot escape their relation with the total social capital. The worker is not obliged to exchange his/her labour power with the wage of a *particular* capitalist, but is obliged to exchange his/her labour power with the wage of *a* capitalist. This is the social nature of exploitation in capitalism. But this form of exploitation is invisible at an interpersonal level, where the worker seems to depend only on the particular capital that employs him/her and interpersonal relations seems to be socially unconstrained and governed simply by competition.

Ontologically, the total social capital is not merely the sum of autonomous individual capitals. Its existence does not depend on the particular individual capitals that constitute it. Rather, it is a general and necessary consequence of the divorce of workers from the means of production, a divorce that subordinates workers' existence to their ability to establish a relation with capital. Of course, in each concrete wage relation, the worker puts his/her labour power under the control of only one piece of the total social capital. But if the worker has to accept these conditions – if he/she must sell his/her labour power – it is because of his/her relation with the total social capital. Therefore, it is the latter that has an autonomous existence with respect to its single constituents, not vice versa. Its development is not merely the aggregate result of a multitude of isolated relations between individual workers and individual capitals in competition with one another. On the contrary, it is the general development of the class relation between capital and labour that conditions the single relations between the members of these opposing classes.

By focusing only on isolated relations between single capitalists and single workers, there is no way to understand the general relations that govern all of them. On the contrary, the impression is that these isolated relations are socially unconstrained and can thus develop according to all thinkable paths. This is the origin of the mystified representation of capitalism developed by bourgeois economists, who do not start their investigation with an analysis of the conditions of social reproduction and do not even accept the existence of the total social capital, but start rather with abstract interpersonal relations in a social vacuum – the fisher and the hunter, Robinson and Friday or, in the literature on power, the talented capitalist and the lazy worker – as if the relationship between the individual capitalist and the individual worker were independent from the general laws of this mode of production based on capital.

The fact that, in competition, the worker can leave the individual capital that employs him/her whenever he/she wishes becomes all that matters in this mystified conception. The other side of the coin, however, is that, if he/she really does it, he/she will simply have to find another individual capital willing to employ him/her. As Marx (1847A, ch. 2) said:

> The worker leaves the capitalist, to whom he has sold himself, as often as he chooses, and the capitalist discharges him as often as he sees fit … But the worker … cannot leave the whole class of buyers, i.e., the

capitalist class, unless he gives up his own existence. He does not belong to this or that capitalist, but to the capitalist class; and it is for him to find his man – i.e., to find a buyer in this capitalist class.

The worker is free from any individual capital, but tied to total social capital, as its accessory. This is the peculiarity of capitalist coercion: 'The Roman slave was held by fetters: the wage laborer is bound to his owner by invisible threads' (Marx 1867, ch. 23).

The role of total social capital in this mode of production is not only a matter of logical necessity. As Marx (1857, Notebook 7) notices, the general character of capital appears also empirically as the capital of a nation or of a geographic area. The exchange rate between two currencies is one of the empirical manifestations of the existence of total social capital. This relative price of one currency in terms of another affects all individual capitals of the countries involved, no matter their degree of autonomy within each country. It is a direct relation between the total social capital of two nations.

The origins of competition

The development of total social capital as an autonomous ontological entity is the key to understand the origins and the development of competition and its transformation into a coercing mechanism. As Marx (1857, Notebook 4) explains, 'Conceptually, *competition* is nothing other than the inner *nature of capital,* its essential character, appearing in and realised as the reciprocal interaction of many capitals with one another, the inner tendency as external necessity. (Capital exists and can only exist as many capitals, and its self-determination therefore appears as their reciprocal interaction with one another)'.

Competition is not universal and everlasting as it may appear to an observer within the capitalist mode of production. Instead, its historical development is an integral part of the development of capital and its apparently universal nature is simply a consequence of the generalisation of this new mode of production based on capital.

Analytically, the first economic category that explains the origins of economic competition is private property. In Engels' (1844) words:

We have seen that in the end everything comes down to competition, so long as private property exists ... because private property isolates everyone in his own crude solitariness, and because, nevertheless, everyone has the same interest as his neighbour, one landowner stands antagonistically confronted by another, one capitalist by another, one worker by another. In this discord of identical interests resulting precisely from this identity is consummated the immorality of mankind's condition hitherto; and this consummation is competition.

Private property alone, however, cannot explain the central role of competition in capitalism. In fact, it is only when private property becomes capitalistic private property that competition becomes *the* coordinating mechanism of this mode of production.

In capitalism, property is characterised not only by its legal form as private property, but also by its unequal distribution between the two classes of capitalists and wage workers. And, ultimately, it is this unequal distribution that pushes the two classes on opposite sides of the labour market. Property relations are thus also class relations in capitalism (Campbell, 1993). The distribution of individual property can change over time, but these changes remain internal to class relations: one individual gets richer, the other poorer but, from the viewpoint of society, these changes simply reproduce a class of proprietors and a class of propertyless, a class of buyers and a class of sellers of labour power.

At a social level, capitalistic private property may thus be defined simply as the separation of the means of production from the workers and as the corresponding monopoly by the capitalist class. This social notion of property is invariant with respect to changes in individual property. Such a dual nature of private property – its individual variance and social invariance – is not accidental in capitalism. It is, on the contrary, an essential feature of this mode of production, a necessary condition for its reproduction. Changes in the distribution of individual property and reproduction of class property are two faces of the same coin (Chattopadhyay 1994).

Marx discusses at length the process of commodification of labour power and the parallel shaping of private property between social classes. He explains that for the wage–labour relation to arise the worker must be both legally free to sell his/her labour power and economically dependent on this sale (Marx 1867, ch. 6). Then, he discusses the historical circumstances that produced 'on the one side owners of money or commodities, and on the other men possessing nothing but their own labour power', and the mechanisms that reproduce these classes of people.[2]

The development of capitalistic private property and the development of competition are parts of the same process and mutually reinforce each other: private property puts individuals against one another and unleashes rivalry behaviours; competition, with its economic incentives, contributes to develop and generalise property relations. Here, however, Marx and Engels take two slightly different theoretical routes.

Engels (1844, 1884) intends to show that all the categories of political economy and the realities to which they correspond presuppose both competition and private property. In his critique, however, he explains competition as a consequence of private property, but his treatment of the origins of private property remains mainly of a historical character.

It is Marx that undertakes the task of explaining also logically the origins of private property (Clarke 1991). In fact, particularly in his early writings, Marx focuses on the relations of private property to another social relation, namely alienated labour, which suggests a more articulated relation between private property and competition. As he explains, in order for labour to be appropriated in the form of property, it must first take the form of alienated labour. In this sense, 'although private property appears as the basis and cause of alienated labour, it is in fact its consequence ... Later, however, this relationship becomes reciprocal' (Marx 1844).

Put another way, Marx arrives at his social conception of competition via its relations with alienated labour, as a category that logically precedes private property. Engels focuses instead on the necessarily asymmetrical distribution of private property between social classes as condition of reproduction of this mode of production. But, for both of them, commodification of labour power is the theoretical and historical reason for the class nature of competition in capitalism.[3]

Competition and the contradictions of capital

By enforcing capital laws, competition imposes the contradictory nature of capital on society. This contradictory nature manifests itself on both sides of the capital–labour relationship.

As already mentioned, Marx's discussion of competition in *Capital* begins with one of the central conflicts between capital and labour: the length of the working day. Within the working class, workers are forced to cheapen their labour power and maximise their effort at work and the length of the working day. These are the conditions for being hired that competition dictates on workers. Similarly, within the capitalist class, competition forces individual capitalists to extract as much labour as possible from workers' labour power: not so much because of their subjective desire, but because of the objective needs of capital. Marx (1867, ch. 10) writes:

> *Après moi le déluge!* is the watchword of every capitalist and of every capitalist nation. Hence Capital is reckless of the health or length of life of the labourer, unless under compulsion from society. To the outcry as to the physical and mental degradation, the premature death, the torture of over-work, it answers: Ought these to trouble us since they increase our profits? But looking at things as a whole, all this does not, indeed, depend on the good or ill will of the individual capitalist. Free

competition brings out the inherent laws of capitalist production, in the shape of external coercive laws having power over every individual capitalist.

It is not an ethical question of 'good or ill will', but the necessary condition for minimising costs and remaining in business. This is the 'essential locomotive force of the bourgeois economy' as Marx calls it in the *Grundrisse*. But, in doing so, competition also tends to deteriorate labour power, to the point of becoming an obstacle to capital accumulation. 'The unnatural extension of the working day ... shortens the length of life of the individual labourer, and therefore the duration of his labour power'. This raises the costs of its reproduction 'just as in a machine the part of its value to be reproduced every day is greater the more rapidly the machine is worn out'. Without forces capable to counterbalance competition, the imperative of exploitation produces a tendency towards 'over-exploitation'. As a car that is driven excessively and runs out of fuel before getting to the next gas station, capital tends to 'over-exploit' labour power and deteriorate its ability to reproduce itself.

The contradictory nature of capital does not manifest itself only in the way it treats living labour, but also in the way it treats dead labour. Competition between capitalists tends to increase constant capital, both in absolute terms and in relation to variable capital. Over time, the valorisation of constant capital by living labour tends to become more and more problematic. This is perhaps the most contentious consequence of competition in Marxist debates. According to Marx, in the same way as competition stimulates technical progress, growth and capital accumulation, it also leads the system to stagnation and crisis. Let us see how.

In the attempt to increase his own profit, under the pressure of competition, every single capitalist gets pushed to innovate, to introduce more advanced technologies and to exploit better increasing returns to scale and the division of labour. Risk aptitude, predictive ability and other subjective considerations are characteristic factors influencing the strategies of individual capitalists. But the general imperative is common to all of them: 'Accumulate, accumulate! That is Moses and the prophets!' (Marx 1867, ch. 24).

After competition has pushed individual capitals to revolutionise the labour process and the organisation of production, it continues its action by generalising these changes to the whole economy. Once a capitalist develops an innovation, there is no real choice for competitors: either they follow, or they get forced out of the market. In this process, innovating firms make higher profits, accumulate faster and increase their market shares at the expense of small capitals, incapable of taking the pace of competition. Capital tends thus to concentrate not so much as a result of subjective choices by capitalists, but as a consequence of the coercive law of competition, which imposes each individual capital to grow, in order not to die.

Such a process of concentration of capital is further reinforced by the tendency for mergers and take-overs that accompanies capitalist accumulation. In analysing these processes, Marx (1867, ch. 25) considers the integral role played by the credit system and the acceleration prompted by crisis. The effect of these processes of concentration and centralisation is that fewer and fewer capitalists control larger and larger capitals. As a result, the competitive process has a tendency towards market power and monopoly.

To the extent that these processes increase the organic composition of capital in the economy, the average profit rate decreases (*ceteris paribus* on the rate of exploitation). The invisible hand of competition shows here the contradictory nature of capital accumulation: the same profit motive behind the success of innovating capitals is in facts the cause of the crisis of capital as a whole. Individual rationality and systemic irrationality are two aspects of capital rationale.

The rise of the organic composition of capital and the fall of the profit rate are heavily disputed topics within Marxian political economy. During the classical period, the fall of the profit rate was generally accepted on empirical grounds. The problem was not to prove it empirically, but to explain it theoretically. After Marx's theoretical contribution, however, some critics and supporters of his ideas have interpreted his notion of tendency mainly empirically, as a description of actual economic processes. Some of them have even attempted to dismiss or defend his theory simply by means of empirical tests.[4]

In my attempt to develop Marx's conception, however, the problem is not strictly empirical but first of all theoretical. Although economic tendencies can be studied for their effects in the empirical realm, in Marx's conception, they do not coincide with their empirical manifestations, but simply govern actual economic processes. Their essential role in this mode of production is not proven by the economic processes that actually develop but by the fact that they emanate directly from the contradictions of capital.

In the study of 'The law of the tendency of the profit rate to fall' (the title of part 3 of volume 3 of *Capital*), Marx's method is straightforward. He examines first 'The law as such' (ch. 13), then the 'counteracting influences' (ch. 14) and, finally, 'The internal contradictions of the law' (ch. 15). By means of this method, he explains this tendency as a structural necessity of the capitalist mode of production and analyses how it interacts with other contingent forces in concrete economic processes. There is no attempt to suggest a typical mechanical pattern towards the crisis or to indicate the inevitable fate of capitalism. On the contrary, Marx shows how competition can actualise this tendency in different ways, but cannot violate the law as such.[5]

The development of competition and the process of capital subsumption

From the viewpoint of the labour process, the process of capital accumulation is also a process of subsumption of the labour process under capital. This process is guided by competition and reinforces the role of competition in this mode of production.

Marx (1864) distinguishes between formal and real subsumption. The former occurs when capital restructures pre-existing non-capitalist working processes without transforming the concrete activity of the worker: capital imposes its logic on the labour process and allows its owner to appropriate the surplus value produced by the worker. This type of surplus value stems from a surplus labour that already existed before the transition to proper capitalistic production. Although the worker concretely continues the same job, his/her surplus labour goes now to a capitalist rather than to a feudal lord.

The latter occurs when capital puts labour concretely under its command, by re-organising the labour process according to capitalistic principles and by transforming and reshaping the tasks of the worker and his/her way of working.

In the development of the capitalist mode of production, Marx argues that formal subsumption tends to become real over time. Only under conditions of simple reproduction can the labour process repeat itself perpetually. Capitalism, however, is an intrinsically dynamic system requiring expansion, which produces a series of well-known consequences: technology is continuously innovated; cheaper processes of production replace old, less competitive, processes; large capitals exploit economies of scale better than small capitals. In these processes, governed by competition, workers' tasks evolve to fit the organising principles of capital. Their concrete work gets reformed in various possible ways. In some cases, the worker himself/herself becomes an appendage of the machine. Against these tendencies, the individual worker has no effective means of resistance. He/she may destroy or sabotage the machine – the concrete commodity that dictates him/her the tasks and the pace of work – but cannot abolish competition, the external force that governs these processes.

In the history of capitalism, competition has directed the process of capital subsumption along two main trajectories. First, it has led capital to develop extensively (so-called globalisation processes) by overcoming national frontiers and by imposing its logic on areas that were not yet subjugated to capital. Second, within a given geographical area, it has pushed capital to develop intensively (commodification processes), by putting more and more aspects of nature and human activity under its control: under the pressure of competition, land, minerals, vegetal and animal life, health, education, culture, sport, science, everything tends to be converted into a commodity.

Although Marx's focused on the economic aspects of capital subsumption, the latter is not restricted to the labour process but applies to the whole sphere of social interaction. As capital subsumes society, competition develops out of the strict economic realm. It is no longer within the strict boundaries of the production process that it imposes the coercing laws of capital, but within social life in general. Competition becomes in this way the general coercing and coordinating mechanism of the whole society.

Of course, there is no automatism in these tendencies. Formal and real subsumption, globalisation and commodification may be reinforced, contrasted or simply directed towards particular trajectories by institutional arrangements, economic policies and subjective choices. However, these attempts at governing capitalist development cannot abolish competition as the internal engine of capital self-expansion.

Association against competition

Against the 'sharpest weapon of the bourgeoisie' (competition), Marx and Engels' (1848) reply is political: 'Working men of all countries, unite!' are the last words of the *Communist manifesto*. Association is in many respects the opposite of competition. It tries to unite people as a way to resist the tendency of competition to isolate them. Unlike competition, however, this mechanism is not really necessary to the reproduction of the capitalist mode of production and its concrete working depends on class consciousness and political action. This is why Marx and Engels discuss workers' association mainly in their studies of concrete social formations and in their political works, where association takes the form of a conscious subjective response to the objective coercive law of competition (Marx 1847A, 1867; Engels 1844, 1845, 1847; Marx and Engels 1848).

Association can be a response to competition within both sides of the capital–labour relationship. But this does not surely come without political struggle, in particular when workers' association is at stake. The concrete development of association in this mode of production is in fact conditioned by the asymmetric power relationship between classes. It is not historically accidental that associations emerged quite spontaneously (and legally) among capitalists, whilst encountered many obstacles among workers and had to remain secret for quite some time. In fact, the right to associate is itself a political victory of the workers' movement, a result of class struggle

– a result that can never be considered definitive and that can be put into question by employers at any time, if class relations allow them to do it.

Notice also that, in the concrete working of capitalism, in some cases workers' association may have stabilising effects. As David Harvey (2010) points out, in their attempt to protect themselves from the coercive law of competition, workers sometimes manage to impose regulations on the way, the forms and the pace of extraction of labour from their labour power. By defending their individual and class interests, they help thus solving the contradiction that we have already examined arising from the tendency to over-exploit their labour power.

But workers' association is not simply the means to contrast the coercive role of competition. It is also the goal of a new society, finally liberated from private property and competition. As Marx and Engels write: 'In place of the old bourgeois society, with its classes and class antagonisms, we shall have an association, in which the free development of each is the condition for the free development of all' (Marx and Engels 1848, ch. 2). 'What will this new social order [communism] have to be like? ... It will, in other words, abolish competition and replace it with association' (Engels 1847, question N. 14).

Of course, Marx and Engels did not have in mind a free association of small property owners, like Proudhon (1847) envisaged, but a free association of producers collectively owning their means of production. These different conceptions of association are, in fact, a direct consequence of their different conceptions of competition. Proudhon did not see competition as a historical mechanism developing with the development of the capitalist mode of production – a consequence of private property and its extension to labour power – but as a universal necessity. As he affirmed, 'there can be no question here of destroying competition, as impossible as to destroy liberty' (Proudhon 1847 ch. 5). Marx, by contrast, analysed competition for its role in the capitalist mode of production and criticised 'Socialist competition' as a contradiction in terms (Deutscher 1952). In his view, the fact that competition may appear as a natural form of human interaction is itself the product of capitalist development. The formation of a competitive human nature is part of the historical process of commodification of labour power and reaches a full development with the generalisation of the process of subsumption of all social relations under capital.

Marx (1847B, ch. 2, part 3) writes: 'M. Proudhon does not know that all history is nothing but a continuous transformation of human nature'. The problem, therefore, is not to explain how God or an immutable human nature produced capitalism, but to understand how, historically, capital has imposed its logic on society and has led to develop a competitive human nature, as the specific human nature of the capitalist mode of production, in the same way as other modes of production shaped completely different human natures in the past.[6]

Against Proudhon, who saw association as a complement to the eternity of competition, a remedy to its inconveniences, Marx and Engels suggest to develop association against competition, as a means to fight against its coercing role and possibly abolish it.

The end of competition

The role of competition in the historical development of capitalism is one of the main lines of development of Marx's critique after his death. Authors such as Hilferding, Karl Kautsky, Nikolai Bucharin, Rosa Luxemburg and Lenin have analysed the historical development of competition and the empirical tendencies towards market power and monopoly. According to Lenin (1917, ch. 1), 'this transformation of competition into monopoly is one of the most important – if not the most important – phenomena of modern capitalist economy'. In Europe, this process has radically transformed the industrial structure and, since the beginning of the twentieth century, cartels and monopolies are already the dominant market forms.

Like industrial and commercial enterprises, banks are subject to the same processes of concentration and centralisation. These tendencies towards market power in industry and finance are reinforced by a tendency towards reciprocal penetration between the two sectors: through crossed acquisition of shares and crossed appointments of directors in the supervisory board of banks and enterprises, capitals tend to unite under a centralised direction. Planning and explicit coordination of economic activities supersede the old system of decentralised entrepreneurial decisions. At this stage, banks take an explicit coordinating role in industrial policy. Their strategies are no longer confined to take a rent from single enterprises. It is now possible to coordinate and plan the activity of whole industrial sectors or even of the whole economy.

The spread of monopolies and the fusion of banks and industry characterise the rise of 'finance capital', which historically has transformed the ordinary working of capitalism by putting it under the supervision of a financial oligarchy. Monopoly and cartels are now the rule and capitalism has reached its 'highest stage' – imperialism – in which finance capital imposes its dominion on the economy (Lenin 1917).

The consequences of this transformation in the mode of coordination of individual capitals has been longly debated within Marxism. Kautsky (1914) interpreted this process of monopolisation as a tendency to end economic and political rivalry. In his 'ultra-imperialist' conception, he suggests that, after the monopolisation of the economy, the tendency of competition to create monopoly will lead the great imperialist powers to federate and end their arms race. It is Hilferding (1910) however that develops more accurately the economic aspects of this conception. In his view, the processes of capital concentration and centralisation will inevitably lead to the formation of a 'general cartel'. At that point, a single body will consciously regulate the whole of capitalist production and the volume of production in all branches of industry, which *de facto* will abolish competition and its coordinating role in the economy. In the Marxist debate, this idea that monopoly eliminates competition and alters the mechanisms of capital accumulation has been very influential, in particular within the 'monopoly capital school' (Sweezy 1942, Baran 1957, Baran and Sweezy 1966, 2012, Foster 1986, Foster and Szlajfer 1984 eds).[7]

This conception, however, raises two problems. The first one is empirical. The general assumption is that there exists an empirical relation between competition and monopoly, according to which the former is inexorably superseded by the latter. Monopoly capitalism would then be a predetermined destiny of this mode of production. This, however, is neither entirely consistent with the actual development of capitalism, nor with Marx's conception. Indeed, Marx points out a number of counter-tendencies produced by competition, which interact with the main tendencies towards concentration and centralisation. He argues that the empirical development of monopolistic market forms is not a unidirectional process but the result of a dialectical relation between these tendencies and counter-tendencies. This explains the complex dynamics that characterise empirically the evolution of market forms. The empirical limits of a mechanical conception of monopolisation are recognised also within the monopoly capital tradition. Paul Sweezy (2004), in particular, points out that the breakup of existing firms and the founding of new ones, under the pressure of competition, have historically 'prevented the formation of anything even remotely approaching Hilferding's general cartel'.

The second problem is theoretical. Does the rise of monopolistic market forms really abolish competition? Clearly, if competition is understood simply as a market form, the answer is almost tautological: giant corporations cannot exist in perfectly competitive markets. If however competition is conceived of as a coordinating and coercive mechanism that develops with the development of capital, the answer is less obvious. As Lenin (1917, ch. 7) argues, these transformations of the dominant market forms and the rise of a new financial oligarchy are internal to the capitalist mode of production. Imperialism does not supersede capitalism, it is only a special stage of it: 'The monopolies, which have grown out of free competition, do not eliminate the latter, but exist above it and alongside it'.

Monopoly and imperialism are not the empirical proof that competition has disappeared but rather the opposite. They are the manifestation of the development of competition as a coercive mechanism, which imposes single capitals to grow, to merger and to struggle with other capitals at higher and higher levels of capital concentration. Competition is not a temporary or accidental feature of capitalism, but its essential coordinating mechanism. Imperialism narrows the empirical role of competitive markets but does not erase competition as the mechanism that links individual capitals. Competition as a market form becomes an exception but its role as a coordinating and coercive mechanism develops at a higher stage.

Lenin is also aware of the scientific and political risks hidden behind a distorted and mystified account of competition as merely a market form. With the development of monopolies and financial oligarchies, he notices, a mystified conception of competition develops as well. The ills of capitalism are not sought in its internal logic, in its general and necessary governing mechanisms, but in its particular and occasional developments. Monopoly and imperialism are not conceived of as intrinsic products of capitalist accumulation, but as annoying violations of competition. Finance capital is not understood as a higher stage of capital accumulation but as a detriment of the accumulation of industrial capital.

In the political debate, this mystified conception suggests a defence of competition and industry and a condemnation of monopoly and finance: the former appear as socially desirable and the latter as their socially undesirable distortions: '"on these grounds" reactionary, petty-bourgeois critics of capitalist imperialism dream of going *back* to "free", "peaceful", and "honest" competition' (Lenin 1917, ch. 1). But 'the aim of proletarian policy cannot today be the ideal of restoring free competition – which has now become a reactionary ideal – but the complete elimination of competition by the abolition of capitalism' (Lenin 1917, ch. 9).

Bourgeois economics and the myth of perfect competition

With the development of capitalism and the subsumption of society under capital, social goals, moral norms, traditions, customs and habits give way to commodity production and 'cash payment'. Production becomes only a matter of profit seeking, and individuals – the methodological starting point of modern bourgeois economics – become nothing else but means of capital valorisation. Only at this stage can competition appear as natural. Competition becomes part of the spontaneous way of individuals to relate to their fellows. It becomes a social standard, a normative benchmark, in every act of social life, far beyond the realm of commodity production. It becomes natural to compete at school, in physical activities, in art, in writing books.

And for the scientist it becomes finally possible to conceive of a world entirely regulated by market relations and competition.

This explains how the general equilibrium model has become the intellectual reference of mainstream economics. Atomised individuals competing in the market are not seen as the product of centuries of capitalistic relations, but as the ultimate cause of all economic phenomena. Competition is emptied of its history, of its social nature and of its coercive content and presented as a universal mode of interaction and, at the same time, as the highest expression of human freedom.

Since its appearance, the general equilibrium model received great attention in the scientific community. Walras' works were translated into Italian and German and became rapidly influential in academic research (although the French economist never got an academic chair in his country). Like the theories of Stanley Jevons and Carl Menger – the other founders of the so called marginal revolution – his model was a sophisticated attempt to provide a harmonious representation of capitalism and represented a clear academical response to the political danger of Marxism. In this new approach, exploitation and class struggle simply disappear as a consequence of methodological individualism, which negates the existence of social classes as real entities of capitalism. Without any direct critique of Marx's theory, neoclassical economics simply rejects its categories by means of methodological assumption.

Notwithstanding the efforts of the best mathematical economists, it took several decades before this research led to rigorous results. In the meantime, however, perfect competition had almost disappeared from real capitalism, as a result of the processes of concentration and centralisation, driven precisely by the competitive mechanism. Historically, these processes developed very rapidly, without any consideration for the slow progress in mathematics by neoclassical economists. As the debate on imperialism shows, few decades after its initial formulation, the general equilibrium model had already become, too say the least, anachronistic.

And when rigorous theoretical results finally arrived, it was all but a success. As we have seen, the solution of the model showed in fact the internal contradictions of this conception of competition, not its scientific validity. In economics teaching, it is now customary to deal with Arrow-Debreu's solutions of the problem of existence and Pareto optimality of a general equilibrium. Less popular are instead the negative results on stability and uniqueness, which deprive the model of any practical utility and interpretative power.

Paradoxically, it is precisely when the general equilibrium paradigm arrived at its empirical and theoretical dead end that it became hegemonic academically, as exemplified by the award of the Nobel prize to Arrow, in

1972, and to Debreu, in 1983. And the paradox in the paradox is that before the *Royal Swedish academy of social sciences* rewarded the latter for his contributions on the issues of existence and Pareto optimality, the author had already contributed to demonstrate the limits of the entire approach with his analysis of stability and uniqueness.

But these paradoxes are only about economic theory. Politically, these are the years of the rise of the neoliberal doctrine. Any theory apparently supporting workers' 'flexibility', privatisations, liberalisations, deregulations, free movements of capitals and the triumph of competition is now absolutely welcome. Realism and internal consistency are no longer necessary. The goal is not to understand the role of competition in capitalism, but to show that it is beneficial for the individual. Hypotheses and methodological choices do not need to be scrutinised critically. Only their implications matter: competition is ethically just (distribution according to marginal productivity), economically efficient (welfare theorems), and incompatible with all forms of power and coercion (dichotomy power – perfect competition).[8] These are the scientific proofs that perfect competition is the best thing in the world. Even if the model is unrealistic and inconsistent.

Of course, if this conception remained in the mind of the economist and in academic journals, it would not have a serious impact on real economic processes. Thanks to the social prestige of science and to its relations with politics and culture, however, this 'scientific' conception reinforces the appearance that competition is not only natural but also socially desirable.

The definition of criteria of social desirability in social sciences is a highly problematic issue. In a Marxist perspective, there exists no social desirability in societies based on class relations and exploitation, but only class interests. In this sense, the pretence of bourgeois economics to define normative criteria, by abstracting from class relations, is just a clunky attempt to defend the interest of the capitalist class, in the name of social good and political neutrality. The bourgeois economist only performs as an apologist of this system of exploitation. His economic theory contributes to the ideological reproduction of the bourgeois standpoint and to impose it on the whole society as a normative guide: class struggle is nonsense in this conception; it is non-scientific because it cannot be neutral. Competition is the only neutral and natural way of regulating social relations. Its social desirability is not a matter of class interest, but one of economic efficiency.

The imposition of competitive relations as the imperative of society is a long and conflicting process involving both ideological and material production and is ultimately itself part of the process of class struggle. The economist is only one of the players in this process. But, historically, the myth of competition has become a sort of *pensée unique* thanks to the active engagement of politics at a national and an international level. The sharpest weapon of the bourgeoisie is now in the hands of international institutions and national governments wishing to reshape the whole spectrum of economic relations in the name of competition. Political confrontation between right and left wing is obsolete in this mystified conception. According to the neoliberal hegemony, society can only genuflect in front of competition. In the words of Margaret Thatcher, the iron lady who knew how to deal with workers and political opponents: 'Tina – there is no alternative'.

Conclusions

Let me recap Marx's critical path. Against the bourgeois conception of competition, Marx's scientific critique develops its coercing and contradictory nature in the capitalist mode of production. This critique shows that competition is not a specific mechanism of capitalism, but exists in other modes of production as well. More precisely, as Engels suggests, it exists in all economic system in which private property and the market exist. In capitalism, however, competition assumes a special role, since private property and the market impose their logic on the overall production process. Competition becomes thus the general mechanism regulating this mode of production.

Although Marx did not leave us a systematic exposition of the working of this mechanism of social coordination, its causes and effects are at the core of his analysis of class relations and of his explanation of the inner contradictions of capital. Competition and capital accumulation are dialectically linked and constitute two inseparable aspects of capitalist development. If we focus on the inner nature of capital, the contradiction of capitalist development manifests itself as an opposition between capital self-expansion and the barrier that capital itself erects against further expansion. If we look at the same process from the viewpoint of competition, this contradiction appears as a contrast, within the capitalist class, between individual rationality and class interests: by pushing capitalists to accumulate, competition increases individual profits and stimulates economic development; by enforcing capital laws, however, it also realises the conditions that hinder the process of capital valorisation, compress the general profit rate and lead to economic crisis.

According to Marx and Engels, the historical development of competition is nothing else but the process through which capital accumulation becomes an independent force, detached from the goals of individuals and society. In this process, competition acts as an external coercive law, which imposes capital logic over individual will and defines the margins of subjective choices. From an individual viewpoint, workers and capitalists are free to interact and to stop interacting whenever they wish. At a social level, however, competition guides and constrains their choices according to their role in class relations.

As an invisible hand at the service of capital, competition imposes capital accumulation as the only goal of society. Despite the mystifications of bourgeois economics, an imaginary world of complete markets and perfect competition is not a world in which individuals and society can really express themselves freely, but its opposite: the highest expression of capital autonomy with respect to human needs and aspirations. Individuals' subjective preferences and capital's objective needs are not incompatible in capitalism. Rather, they express the way competition regulates human relations at an interpersonal and a social level.

Against this conception of competition as an ambivalent and contradictory force driving capitalist development, neoclassical economists treat competition as the benchmark of social rationality. Failing to explain its origins, they define it as an everlasting norm towards which all economic relations should conform. The scientific question regarding competition is so transformed from a positive to a normative one by a methodological slight of hand: the problem is not to understand how competition works, but to demonstrate that it works well. According to neoclassical economics, the problems of capitalism are not at all caused by competition, but by the lack of it.

To conclude my critique of competition, let me retrace my reconstruction of Marx's conception in negative terms, as a critique of bourgeois economics. Without any notion of total social capital, bourgeois economics cannot grasp the relation between capital and competition and the specific role of competition in this mode of production. It treats capitalism as an everlasting system and, as a consequence, sees competition as a natural fact, deserving no scientific explanation. It correctly associates competition to the invisible hand that guides capitalist development but fails to understand the contradictory nature of capitalist accumulation and the role of competition in enforcing these contradictions. It dreams of a reign of perfect competition as the best guarantee of individual freedom but cannot see that, in this reign, the only one to be free is capital, which subsumes progressively the whole society. With its individualist methodology, it hides the class nature of competition and the role of 'association' as a political response to competition in class struggle; all it can say about workers' association is that it violates competition. Like in Marxist revisionism, it conceives of competition as a market form and believes that its role ceases with the development of monopoly, rather than with the end of capitalism. The neoclassical normative apparatus, formally pursuing the common good, is in fact a contradictory attempt to support 'scientifically' the sharpest weapon of the bourgeoisie against the proletariat.

In this process of idealisation and sacralisation of competition, neoclassical economics only picks up the baton of old vulgar economics. Like the latter, it 'does practically no more than translate the singular concepts of the capitalists, who are in the thrall of competition, into a seemingly more theoretical and generalised language, and attempt to substantiate the justice of those conceptions' (Marx 1894, ch. 13). But this is only the academia. If Thatcher really acted in the interests of the whole society, I let the British miners to judge. And if there is really no alternative, it will be the anticapitalist movement to decide.

Notes

1 Many methodological contributions in this direction have been inspired by the controversy on value theory and the so-called transformation problem (for instance, Mattick 1959, Mosley 1993, Carchedi 1993).
2 Marx dedicates the whole Part VIII of *Capital 1*, to study the process of 'primitive accumulation' and the divorce of the worker from the means of production and harshly criticises the authors that he calls 'vulgar economists' for their abstract speculations on the origin of capitalism. Unfortunately, as we have seen in the first part of the book, the same speculative method, based on hypothetical spontaneous interactions between isolated individuals, has today become the distinguishing feature of new institutionalism and post Walrasian economics.
3 Starting from the recognition of Marx and Engels' slightly different theoretical objectives, Clarke (1994) discusses the different implications of their analysis of competition in the study of crisis.
4 The empirical literature is abundant but mainly focused on the US economy. The debate was opened by Gillman (1957) and the critique of Mage (1963). The relation between Marx's conception and the empirical evidence of capitalist development has been debated by Mandel (1975), Mattick (1972) and Rowthorn (1980). New stimuli to empirical research came then from the development of the Monopoly capital approach and the debate on overaccumulation, underconsumption and profit squeeze (Weisskopf 1979, Wolff 1979, Moseley 1988, 1991, Duménil, Glick and Rangel 1984, 1985, Duménil and Lévy 1993, Sherman 1997, Van Lear 1999, Goldstein 1999, Kleinknecht, Mandel and Wallerstein 1992, Shaikh and Tonak 1994, Brenner 2002). The economy of the UK has been studied by Glyn and Sutcliffe (1972) and Cockshott, Cottrell, and Michaelson (1995). Global studies and international comparisons have been developed by Armstrong, Glyn and Harrison (1984), Glyn (1991) and Shaikh (1999). Recently, the outbreak of the global financial crisis in 2007, has renewed the interest in empirical research (Kotz 2008, Roberts 2009, Kliman 2011, Carchedi and Roberts 2013).
5 The role of competition as the mechanism that actualises these tendencies and that is reinforced – rather than being attenuated – by the development of monopolistic market forms, is developed by Clifton (1977), Shaikh (1978, 1980, 1982), Fine (1982), Weeks (1981, 2010) and Chattopadhyay (2012).

6   Proudhon introduces provocatively the hypothesis of a God in the introduction of his *System of economical contradictions: or, The philosophy of poverty.*
7   This antagonistic relation between monopoly and competition has been criticised by Clifton (1977), Weeks (1981) and Harvey (1999).
8   Although these theoretical results are used as 'scientific' defence of competition, *strictu sensu*, the debate on marginal productivity and the welfare theorems demonstrate in fact the theoretical limits of these theories and the distance of real capitalism from these standards of social desirability.

References

Armstrong, Philip, Andrew Glyn and John Harrison (1984), *Capitalism since world war two*, London, Fontana.
Arthur, Christopher (2002), Capital, competition, and many capitals, in Campbell, Martha and Geert Reuten (eds), *The culmination of capital: Essays on volume 3 of Marx's Capital*, London, Palgrave.
——(2010), Capital in general, *Historical Materialism*, vol. 18, pp. 209–12.
Baran, Paul (1957), *The political economy of growth*, London, Penguin Books.
Baran, Paul and Paul Sweezy (1966), *Monopoly capital: An essay on the American economic and social order*, New York, Monthly Review Press.
——(2012), Some theoretical implications, *Monthly Review*, vol. 64, n. 3. Retrieved from http://monthlyreview.org/2012/07/01/some-theoretical-implications/ (accessed 1 April 2016).
Brenner, Robert (2002), *The boom and the bubble – the US in the world economy*, London, Verso.
Campbell, Martha (1993), Marx's concept of economic relations and the method of *Capital*, in Moseley, Fred (ed.), *Marx's method in 'Capital': A reexamination*, Atlantic Highlands, Humanities Press.
Carchedi, Guglielmo (1993), Marx's logic of inquiry and price formation, in Moseley, Fred (ed.), *Marx's method in 'Capital': A reexamination*, Atlantic Highlands, Humanities Press.
Carchedi, Guglielmo and Michael Roberts (2013), The long roots of the present crisis: Keynesians, Marxians and Marx's law, *World Review of Political Economy*, vol. 4, n. 1, pp. 86–115.
Chattopadhyay, Paresh (1994), The Marxian concept of capital and the Soviet experience, Westport, Praeger.
——(2012), Competition, in Fine, Ben and Alfredo Saad Filho (eds), *The Elgar companion to Marxist economics*, Cheltenham, Edward Elgar Publishing Limited.
Clarke, Simon (1991), Marx, marginalism and modern sociology: From Adam Smith to Max Weber, London, Macmillan.
——(1994), *Marx's theory of crisis*, London, Macmillan.
Clifton, James (1977), Competition and the evolution of the capitalist mode of production, *Cambridge Journal of Economics*, vol. 1, n. 2, pp. 137–51.

Cockshott, Paul, Allin Cottrell and Greg Michaelson (1995), Testing Marx: Some new results from UK data, *Capital and Class*, vol. 19, n. 1, pp. 103–30.

Deutscher, Isaac (1952), *Socialist competition*. Retrieved from www.marxists.org/archive/deutscher/1952/socialist-competition.htm#n2 (accessed 1 March 2016).

Duménil, Gerard, Mark Glick and Jose Rangel (1984), The tendency of the rate of profit to fall in the United States, Part 1, *Contemporary Marxism*, vol. 9, pp. 148–64.

——(1985), The tendency of the rate of profit to fall in the United States, Part 2, *Contemporary Marxism*, vol. 11, pp. 138–52.

Duménil, Gerard and Dominique Lévy (1993), *The economics of the profit rate: Competition, crises, and historical tendencies in capitalism*, Aldershot, Edward Elgar.

Engels, Frederick (1844), *Outlines of a critique of political economy*. Retrieved from www.marxists.org/archive/marx/works/1844/df-jahrbucher/outlines.htm (accessed 1 March 2016).

——(1845), The *conditions of the working-class in England*. Retrieved from www.marxists.org/archive/marx/works/1845/condition-working-class/index.htm (accessed 1 March 2016).

——(1847), *The principles of communism*. Retrieved from www.marxists.org/archive/marx/works/1847/11/prin-com.htm (accessed 1 March 2016).

——(1884), *The origin of the family, private property and the state*. Retrieved from www.marxists.org/archive/marx/works/1884/origin-family/index.htm (accessed 1 March 2016).

Fine, Ben (1982), *Theories of the capitalist economy*, London, Edward Arnold.

Foster, John Bellamy (1986), The theory of monopoly capitalism: An elaboration of Marxian political economy, New York, Monthly Review Press.

Foster, John Bellamy and Henryk Szlajfer (1984 eds), *The faltering economy: The problem of accumulation under monopoly capitalism*, New York, Monthly Review Press.

Gillman, Joseph (1957), *The falling rate of profit: Marx's law and its significance to twentieth-century capitalism*, New York, Dennis Dobson.

Glyn, Andrew (1991), International trends in profitability, in Dunne, Paul (ed.), *Quantitative Marxism*, Cambridge, Polity Press.

Glyn, Andrew and Bob Sutcliffe (1972), *British capitalism, workers and the profit squeeze*, London, Penguin Books.

Goldstein, Jonathan (1999), The simple analytics and empirics of the cyclical profit squeeze and cyclical underconsumption theories: Clearing the air, *Review of Radical Political Economics*, vol. 31, n. 1, pp. 74–88.

Harvey, David (1999), *Limits to Capital*, New York, Verso.

——(2010), *A companion to Marx's 'Capital'*, New York, Verso.

Heinrich, Michael (1989), Capital in general and the structure of Marx's Capital, *Capital and Class*, vol. 13, pp. 63–79.

Hilferding, Rudolf (1910), *Finance capital: A study of the latest phase of capitalist development*. Retrieved from www.marxists.org/archive/hilferding/1910/finkap/index.htm (accessed 1 March 2016).

Kautsky, Karl (1914), *Ultra-imperialism*. Retrieved from www.marxists.org/archive/kautsky/1914/09/ultra-imp.htm (accessed 1 March 2016).

Kleinknecht, Alfred, Ernest Mandel and Immanuel Wallerstein (1992 eds), *New findings in long wave research*, London, Palgrave Macmillan.

Kliman, Andrew (2011), *The failure of capitalist production: Underlying causes of the Great Recession*, London, Pluto press.

Kotz, David (2008), Contradictions of economic growth in the neoliberal era: Accumulation and crisis in the contemporary U.S. economy, *Review of Radical Political Economics*, vol. 40, n. 2, pp. 174–88.

Lenin, Vladimir (1917), *Imperialism, the highest stage of capitalism: A popular outline*. Retrieved from www.marxists.org/archive/lenin/works/1916/imp-hsc/index.htm (accessed 1 March 2016).

Mage, Shane (1963), *The law of the falling tendency of the rate of profit: Its place in the Marxian theoretical system and relevance to the US economy*, Phd Thesis, Columbia University.

Mandel, Ernest (1975), *Late capitalism*, London, NLB.

Marx, Karl (1844), *Economic and philosophic manuscripts*. Retrieved from www.marxists.org/archive/marx/works/1844/manuscripts/preface.htm (accessed 1 March 2016).

——(1847A), *Wage labour and capital*. Retrieved from www.marxists.org/archive/marx/works/1847/wage-labour/index.htm (accessed 1 March 2016).

——(1847B), *The poverty of philosophy*. Retrieved from www.marxists.org/archive/marx/works/1847/poverty-philosophy/index.htm (accessed 1 March 2016).

——(1857), *Outlines of the critique of political economy*. Retrieved from www.marxists.org/archive/marx/works/1857/grundrisse/index.htm (accessed 1 March 2016).

——(1864), *The process of production of capital, Draft chapter 6 of Capital – Results of the direct production process*. Retrieved from www.marxists.org/archive/marx/works/1864/economic/index.htm (accessed 1 March 2016).

——(1867), *Capital: Critique of political economy, vol, 1, The process of capitalist production*. Retrieved from www.marxists.org/archive/marx/works/1867-c1/index.htm (accessed 1 March 2016).

——(1894), *Capital: Critique of political economy, vol, 3, The process of capitalist production as a whole*. Retrieved from www.marxists.org/archive/marx/works/1894-c3/index.htm (accessed 1 March 2016).

Marx, Karl and Frederick Engels (1848), *The communist manifesto*. Retrieved from www.marxists.org/archive/marx/works/1848/communist-manifesto/index.htm (accessed 1 March 2016).

Mattick, Paul (1959), Value theory and capital accumulation, *Science and Society*, vol. 23, pp. 27–51.

——(1972), Ernest Mandel's late capitalism. Retrieved from www.marxists.org/archive/mattick-paul/1972/mandel.htm (accessed 1 March 2016).

Moseley, Fred (1988), The rate of surplus value, the organic composition, and the general rate of profit in the U.S. economy, 1947–67: A critique and update of Wolff's estimates, *American Economic Review*, vol. 78, n. 1, pp. 298–303.

——(1991), *The falling rate of profit in the postwar United States economy*, London, Palgrave Macmillan.

——(1993), Marx's logical method and the 'transformation problem', in Moseley, Fred (ed.), *Marx's method in 'Capital': A reexamination*, Atlantic Highlands, Humanities Press.

Pilling, Geoff (1980), *Marx's Capital, philosophy and political economy*. Retrieved from www.marxists.org/archive/pilling/works/capital/index.htm (accessed 1 March 2016).

Proudhon, Pierre-Joseph (1847), *System of economical contradictions: or, The philosophy of poverty*. Retrieved from www.marxists.org/reference/subject/economics/proudhon/philosophy/index.htm (accessed 1 March 2016).

Roberts, Michael (2009), The Great Recession: Profit cycles, economic crisis. A Marxist View, Lulu Press, eBook.

Rosdolsky, Roman (1977), *The making of Marx's 'Capital'*, London, Pluto Press.

Rowthorn, Bob (1980), *Capitalism, conflict and inflation*, London, Lawrence and Wishart.

Shaikh, Anwar (1978), An introduction to the history of crisis theories, in URPE (eds), *U.S. capitalism in crisis*, New York, URPE.

——(1980), Marxian competition versus perfect competition, *Cambridge Journal of Economics*, vol. 4, n. 1, pp. 75–83.

——(1982), Neo-Ricardian economics: A wealth of algebra, a poverty of theory, *Review of Radical Political Economics*, vol. 14, n. 2, pp. 67–83.

——(1999), Explaining the global economic crisis, *Historical Materialism*, vol. 5, pp. 104–44.

Shaikh, Anwar and Ahmet Tonak (1994), *Measuring the wealth of nations: The political economy of national accounts*, Cambridge, Cambridge University Press.

Sherman, Howard (1997), Theories of cyclical profit squeeze, *Review of Radical Political Economics*, vol. 29, n. 1, pp. 139–47.

Smith, Adam (1776), *An inquiry into the nature and causes of the wealth of nations*. Retrieved from www.gutenberg.org/files/3300/3300-h/3300-h.htm (accessed 1 March 2016).

Sweezy, Paul (1942), *Theory of capitalist development*, London, Dobson books ltd.

——(2004), Monopoly capitalism, *Monthly Review*, vol. 56, n. 5. Retrieved from http://monthlyreview.org/2004/10/01/monopoly-capitalism (accessed 1 March 2016).

Van Lear, William (1999), Profitability in business cycle theory and forecasting, *Review of Radical Political Economics*, vol. 31, n. 2, pp. 46–60.

Weeks, John (1981), *Capital and exploitation*, Princeton, Princeton University Press.

——(2010), *Capital, exploitation and economic crises*, London, Routledge.

Weisskopf, Thomas (1979), Marxian crisis theory and the rate of profit in the postwar U.S. economy, *Cambridge Journal of Economics*, n. 3, pp. 341–78.

Wolff, Edward (1979), The rate of surplus value, the organic composition, and the general rate of profit in the U.S. economy, 1947–67, *American Economic Review*, vol. 69, pp. 329–41.

6 Capitalism as a system of power

Working men of all countries, unite!

(Marx and Engels 1848, ch. 4)

We have now all the elements to develop the relation between social coercion and interpersonal power in capitalism. Marx's critique shows that they act at different ontological levels but have a common cause: capital. The problem is to disentangle the different forms of coercion and power that capital imposes on society and individuals. In this chapter, I put order in these forms of coercion and power, discuss the mechanisms through which they are reproduced, and explain how they appear in the empirical realm. In short, I develop an explicit ontology of coercion and power in the capitalist mode of production.

To develop this ontology, I inspire my critique to the philosophy of 'critical realism'. The latter focuses on the relations between ontology and methodology and defends the primacy of the former over the latter in scientific research. Very simply, methodological choices always presuppose particular ontological assumptions. If reality is supposed to be in a certain way, a certain instrument of investigation might be appropriate. The same instrument, however, might be fallacious if reality is made differently. Starting from this almost trivial consideration, critical realism develops a stratified ontology in which empirical entities are logically separated from the non observable entities that govern them and criticises the approaches based on a flat ontology in which only empirical entries are supposed to exist.

As we have seen, it is precisely this kind of ontological reasoning that allows Marx developing a critique of capital in which the essential forms of social coercion of this mode of production (which remain mostly invisible empirically) are logically separated, but dialectically linked with the forms of power that appear in interpersonal relations (and that are, at least partly, detectable empirically). And conversely the lack of ontological arguments is the cause of the contradictory path followed by the neoclassical approach to power.

Neoclassical economics presupposes an 'empirical realist' ontology wherein, essentially, what is empirically observed is treated as synonymous with what is: it is a kind of 'what you see is what you get' ontology. Marxism, by contrast, presupposes a structured or depth ontology wherein, underlying the empirically observed and the actual occurrences, are social structures and mechanisms that govern them. Put simply, for those like critical realists and Marxists committed to a structured ontology, essence underlies appearance, whereas for neoclassical economists, committed to an empirical realist ontology, appearance is all there is. These two different ontologies, then, motivate and sustain their different methodologies in the research on power.

Let me thus reconsider the basic notions of power developed in the economic debate and their relations with the categories developed in Marx's critique. In general terms, power is *the faculty to do or to not do something*. In social sciences, this kind of power is called 'power to act' (PTA). The economic debate, however, has focused mainly on a different kind of power, existing only in interpersonal relations, namely *the capacity to influence the action of others*, which is generally defined as 'power over somebody' (POS). Whilst both aspects are important, neoclassical economics cannot explain PTA and its relations with POS because of its ontology, and so operates entirely with an analysis restricted to POS. This manifests itself in the literature, via the twofold assumption that the distribution of PTA in society is given and that in a system of perfect (Walrasian) competition there is no power in interpersonal relations. This is because, in perfectly competitive markets, individuals with their inborn endowments can choose among a number of equivalent interpersonal relations. Therefore, if an individual tries to impose his/her will upon another, the latter can simply choose to stop interacting with him/her with no loss, independent on their respective PTAs. In such a context, POS does not exist, no matter the distribution of PTA.

From a Marxists perspective, however, capitalist relations are recognised as, by their nature, power relations. Under capitalism, PTA is asymmetrically distributed in society, and this asymmetry (which is necessary to the day-to-day operation of capitalism and has nothing to do with the particular competitive or non-competitive form of the market) is indeed the cause of relations of POS at an interpersonal level and constitutes an essential aspect of capitalist social coercion.

The reason why Marxism can grasp these forms of social coercion and their relationship with POS, whereas the neoclassical economics cannot, does not lie strictly at the level of theory, but at that of meta-theory. It is

Marxism's ontological presuppositions that discourage the development of theory in terms of isolated individuals, and encourage the development of theory in terms of the relations between agents and the social structures they interact with. And unsurprisingly, some of these social structures are the vehicle through which power is asserted.

I begin by presenting critical realism and its relations with Marxism. Next, I consider the relations between the different forms of power in a critical realist perspective. As well as the actual-empirical notions of PTA and POS, I discuss non-observable entities such as 'constraining and conditioning structures', 'coercing mechanisms', 'counter-powers' and 'systems of power'. The analytical tools that I use to characterise these ontological entities are borrowed from decision theory. Decision theory is the underlying framework of most of the approaches based on methodological individualism, but constitutes in fact a broader framework in which social categories can be discussed as well. Its use facilitates comparisons with neoclassical economics but also allows developing the relations between individual and social categories.[1]

This abstract ontological framework is then used to analyse the concrete forms of economic power in capitalism. The structure of this section is the same of the preceding one. Here, however, PTA, POS, and the other power-related concepts are discussed in the context of capitalist relations as purchasing power, market power, authority, etc. This analysis relies on Marx's critique of capital as a complex ontological entity, characterised by a separation between appearances and essence. My thesis is that capitalism is a system of power, with particular empirical manifestations of an underlying non-observable power structure.

Critical realism

The critical realist movement begins in the philosophical camp with the work of Roy Bhaskar in the 1970s, and is developed in the 1980s thanks to the contributions of Ted Benton, Andrew Collier and William Outhwaite (cf. Norris 1999). Today, critical realism is a movement encompassing different disciplines including economics, sociology, biology and physics.

The growing impact of this movement is witnessed by the number of associations, forums and workshops fostering the discussion and development of critical realism and by the increasing penetration in academic journals of themes related to critical realism. Since 1998, the *International Association for Critical Realism* has published also a specialised journal – the *Journal of Critical Realism*. In the context of philosophy and economics, the works of Margaret Archer (1995), Bhaskar (1978, 1979, 1986, 1991, 1993), Collier (1994), Tony Lawson (1997, 2003), and Outhwaite (1987) constitute some of the main theoretical references. Some essential readings are collected in Archer, Bhaskar, Collier, Lawson and Norrie (1998 eds). Steve Fleetwood (1999 ed.) is a collection of contributions to the debate about critical realism in economics. The development of a critical realist perspective in economics owes much to the 'Cambridge school', strongly influenced by Lawson (some of its contributions have appeared in the *Cambridge Journal of Economics* and in the *Review of Social Economy*).

According to critical realism, neoclassical economics can be characterised by its deductivist methodology, based on closed system modelling. Deductivism, like any other method, presupposes an ontology, in the sense that the nature of reality must be supposed to be such that it can be investigated using the deductivist method.

Although neoclassical economics rarely develops ontological arguments, its implicit ontology consists of atomistic, empirical events. More precisely, reality is supposed to be constituted by two domains, the 'actual' and the 'empirical'. The former consists of events and states of affairs, the latter of human experiences of them. These two domains are supposed to be fused, so that actual events are presumed to coexist with their empirical perceptions. Reality is thus identified with what is perceived, or, at least, what is perceivable under certain conditions, and the explanation of an event is provided by looking at other (perceivable) events, since nothing else exists in this ontology.

If knowledge is, allegedly, gained through observing and recording these events empirically (as data), then generalised and/or scientific knowledge can only be gained if these events produce some kind of stable pattern – if they simply produce a totally random flux of events, on this understanding, there could not be access to knowledge. In fact, the pattern these events produce has to be one of event regularity or constancy. Neoclassical economists, typically, generate these event regularities by assumption. The result is an artificially closed system. The snag is that socio-economic systems are almost always open systems – i.e., systems wherein event regularities are not ubiquitous.

By contrast, according to critical realism, 'the world is composed not only of events and states of affairs and our experiences or impressions of them, but also of underlying structures, powers, mechanisms and tendencies, which exist, whether or not detected, and govern or facilitate actual events' (Lawson 1997, p. 21).

The critical realist ontology is stratified and consists of three domains, the 'empirical', the 'actual' and the 'real' (also called the 'deep'). These three domains are presumed to be out of phase with one another. This means that it is not possible to establish a one-to-one relationship between experiences and events or between events and mechanisms.

This ontology encourages a different methodology from deductivism. In contrast to the deductivist mode of inference, observable events are not explained in terms of other observable events, but in terms of underlying structures, their causal powers, the mechanisms through which they operate and the tendencies that they generate. This move from phenomenal reality to the deep domain is a mode of inference called 'retroduction'. Structures and mechanisms, however, do not necessarily act in isolation; on the contrary, in general, an event or state of affair is governed by the interaction of different structures and mechanisms. The scientific problem is thus to identify the structures and mechanisms that govern phenomenal reality and to explain the forms of their interaction.

These different ontological premises lead to radically different conceptions of power. According to critical realism, power is a notion that refers to entities in the three domains, with PTA and POS being the main visible forms of power in the actual-empirical domain, whose governing invisible mechanisms are however in the deep domain. The methodological problem is thus to explain the relation between the empirical forms of power and the underlying structures and mechanisms. By contrast, in empirical realist inspired theories, the notion of power is restricted to particular empirical phenomena. This leads to a different methodology. In fact, the most common way to study power relations within empirical realism has been to assume atomistic individuals as the sole explanatory units of eventual relations of POS (methodological individualism).

But in order to close the system and make deductivism applicable, atomistic individuals had also to be deprived of any real agency. Methodological individualism has thus been coupled with the assumption of rational economic men. Only such a man is analytically empty, mechanically predetermined, so that there is no intrinsic properties that can change, thereby generating different responses to the same stimuli at different times. Only an atomistically conceived *homo economicus* responds identically, and predictably every single time he is faced with the same set of conditions.[2]

It is within this methodological framework, emanating from the empirical realist ontology, that neoclassical economics has developed its narrow conception of power.

Critical realism and Marxism

The relationship between Marxism and critical realism is not clear cut. Today, there is a growing literature on this subject, which shows the coexistence of different, and at least partly incompatible, viewpoints.

A first, encouraging exploration of this relationship is developed by the founder himself of critical realism, Bhaskar (1991, p. 143), who affirms that 'Marx's work at its best illustrates critical realism; and critical realism is the absent methodological fulcrum of Marx's work'. The compatibility between Marx's analysis and critical realism has been defended at different levels, ranging from a simple formal coherence to a deep meta-theoretical unity. Hans Ehrbar (1998) goes so far as to say that 'Marx was a critical realist, long before critical realism was born', and proposes a sentence-by-sentence translation of Marx's *Capital* into critical realist terms (Ehrbar 2001). The thesis of a mutually helpful relationship is developed, in particular, by Collier (1979, 1989), Sean Creaven (2001, 2003), Fleetwood (2001) and Jonathan Joseph (2001). On the opposite side, some overt criticisms about the compatibility between Marxism and critical realism are developed by Richard Gunn (1989), Kevin Magill (1994) and John Roberts (1999).

The main points of contrast and convergence between Marxism and critical realism are discussed in a book edited by Andrew Brown, Fleetwood and Roberts (2001). In their introductory chapter, the editors explore three different viewpoints. According to Fleetwood, the nature of the relationship between critical realism and Marxism is philosophical. In his view, critical realism can supply an all-encompassing philosophy of science that is missing in Marxism and that allows us to place some Marxian notions on a more secure philosophical footing.

By contrast, Roberts argues that Marxism is in no need of the philosophical services of critical realism and suggests that a more suitable way for Marxism to proceed would be to develop the theoretical categories of historical materialism, rather than incorporate some concepts and categories of critical realism, which, in his view, are incompatible with historical materialism.

Brown thinks that the lesson Marxism can learn from critical realism is the need to articulate the concepts of Marxian theory at the level of generality of philosophy. More precisely, he suggests that a Marxist philosophy should embrace some of the fundamental concepts of critical realism, such as structural causality, the distinction between thought and mind-independent object, the notion of tendencies, the relations between structure and agency. These notions, however, are stressed also within other philosophical perspectives. Thus, Brown sees no particular reason for Marxism to embrace a precisely critical realist philosophy and defends instead a 'materialist dialectics', as an alternative Marxist philosophical position able to embrace and transcend critical realism.

It is not necessary here to go further into the details of the general coherence of Marxism and critical realism. For my purpose, it is sufficient to re-establish the distinguishing features of the capitalist mode of production along with its Marxian critique and interpret them in critical realist terms. This is sufficient to determine the essential forms of social coercion and interpersonal power of capitalism.[3]

The ontology of power

In order to discuss organically the different forms of power within an abstract decision making system, we must first of all define their ontological nature and the relations among them. These definitions can then be used to characterise the intrinsic forms of power of each concrete decision making system. But let me first of all define a 'decision making system' in terms of decision theory, as 1) a set of 'agents', 2) their individual 'decision making sets' and 'goals' and 3) the relations among these individual decision making sets and goals.

Power to act

PTA is defined by the 'decision making set' of the agent, which exhaustively describes its potential courses of action. 'Agents' are not only individuals, but also collective actors (a firm, a bank, a political party, a trade union, a think tank or any other actor capable of taking decisions). There is no reason to assume that they know precisely and take into account rationally their own decision making sets and those of the others. Imperfect information and bounded rationality can lead to partial and imperfect knowledge. Independent of this, however, the sets of actions that agents can and cannot materially undertake *exist* and do not depend on what agents know.

Of course, the analysis of the existing PTA is not sufficient to determine what agents will do, or, to put it differently, the analysis of the *existence* of PTA cannot explain how agents *exercise* it: choices do not depend only on material constraints (or, better, on the perception and interpretation of them), but on goals as well. PTA is only the objective side of the decision making process, the definition of agents' goals being its subjective side.

Agents' goals are defined on the basis of their subjective preferences and their subjective knowledge of the decision making set. Methodological individualism assumes that both these elements are unproblematic: subjective preferences are taken as given and subjective knowledge is assumed to coincide with objective information (or with pieces of it, when information is assumed to be 'imperfect'). In this broader ontological framework, however, first, agent's preferences might be conditioned by other agents' behaviour and/or by the social context and, second, information is ontologically different from knowledge: the former regards the decision making system as it exists objectively and the latter its subjective perception and interpretation by the agents interacting in the decision making system.[4] Concretely, this means that the same information may be interpreted differently by different agents and lead to different knowledge and different goals even if agents' subjective preferences coincide.

Operationally, at a given moment of time, a measure of the *existing* PTAs is defined by the range of actions inscribed in each individual decision making set. This measure is *ex ante* in the sense that it refers to the means at one's disposal for the exercise of power, not to the exercise of power itself: purchasing power is determined by wealth, not by actual purchases; military power is determined by fire potential, not by the tons of bombs actually dropped. When a power is *exercised*, its measurement is *ex post*. As concerns existence, this measure is a mere imperfect proxy for the *ex ante* measure: purchases are correlated with wealth, bombs with fire potentials, but there is no necessary causality between them. Therefore, even remaining within the actual-empirical domain, empirical correlation is not an adequate tool for the analysis of *existence* of this form of power.

Power over somebody

A has power over *B* when the choice of *B* depends on the specific action chosen by *A* within its own decision making set. This can occur in two cases: first, when *A* has some control of *B*'s decision making set (in this case, POS can be seen as the ability to *change* the PTA of other agents), and, second, when *A* is able to influence *B*'s goals (by conditioning either its preferences or its knowledge). The first case describes the forms of objective POS, the second characterises the forms of subjective POS.

Objective POS and PTA are intimately linked, since the emergence of the former depends on the distribution of the latter in the decision making system. In a system of complex interpersonal relations, agents' decision making sets are necessarily interdependent. In this sense, the forms of objective POS are only the tip of the iceberg that emerges from a sea of asymmetric PTA relations. The strongest form of objective POS is the 'authority relation', in which *A* can order *B* to do something and *B* must obey: in terms of constraints, *A*'s authority over *B* is expressed by *A*'s ability to restrict *B*'s decision making set to just one option.[5]

Subjective POS depends on the ability of an agent to condition the goals of another agent. Methodological individualism excludes, by assumption, this form of power. In a complex system of social interaction, however, the definition of agent's goal is necessarily a social process in which external conditioning cannot be excluded. The strongest form of goal conditioning is 'manipulation', in which *A* is able to determine univocally *B*'s goals.

Operationally, an *ex ante* measure of the *existing* relations of POS must be defined along at least two dimensions, an extensive one and an intensive one. The former is given by the number of agents whose behaviour depends on the action undertaken by A. The latter is given by the kind of consequences of A's choice on other agents' goals and constraints. These dimensions are conceptually independent: on the one hand, it is possible that A has power over many agents but that its power over each of them is weak; on the other hand, it is possible that A has power over only an agent but that this power relation takes its strongest form, namely authority (for objective POS) or manipulation (for subjective POS).

Ex post measures cannot be provided for subjective POS since, conceptually, the origins of B's goals cannot be detected after B has taken its decision. Only B may know whether it would have acted differently if A did not influence its goals. But there is no empirical way for an external observer to prove that this conditioning effectively occurred or that, conversely, B's goals were genuinely developed in isolation by B itself (like methodological individualists suppose). For objective POS, ex post measures can be provided only when the constraints imposed by A on the decision making set of B are binding, given B's goals. If, on the contrary, A modifies B's constraints, but B does not change its choice, this relation of POS cannot be detected by the empirical observation of B's behaviour. These restrictions on the logical detectability of POS imply that empirical analysis can at best reveal a modest sub-set of the existing relations of POS.

The constraining structure

The set of individual decision making sets and their interdependencies define the objective elements of a decision making system. These objective elements can take different forms in terms of set theory. In some cases, individual decision making sets can be incommensurable, in the sense that A can undertake action x, but not action y, whilst B can chose y but not x. In other cases, B's decision making set can be a subset of A's, which is to say that B is more constrained than A (A can undertake actions that are precluded to B). This asymmetry may take different forms and degrees and may regard few agents in the decision making system or all of them. When such an asymmetry exists, at whatever degree, the structure of the decision making system is essentially a 'constraining structure': even if A has no direct power over B, A is structurally less constrained than B.

With this term, I stress the asymmetric *constraints* that the structure of the decision making system imposes on different agents. On the other hand, however, this structure can also be understood as *enabling* individual behaviours that could not be undertaken without its existence. These are just the two sides of the same coin, observed from the angles of asymmetric constraints or asymmetric PTAs.

Unlike PTA and POS, which are attributed to particular agents, the constraining structure is social in nature. The existence of a constraining structure is a signal of the existence of objective forms of social coercion, which can be grasped only by an inspection of the whole decision making system and which remain invisible when the analysis is developed on single interpersonal relations in isolation.

The conditioning structure

The set of individual goals and their interdependencies define the subjective elements of the decision making system. Like in the discussion of objective constraints, these subjective elements can take different forms. In some cases, A's and B's goals might be the product of independent subjective preferences and different interpretative frameworks of available information. In other cases, they might be defined from similar or even coincident preferences and interpretative frameworks. This similarity may be more or less pronounced and may regard few agents in the decision making system or all of them. When such a uniformity in preferences and interpretative frameworks exist, the structure of the decision making system is essentially a 'conditioning structure'.

Like the constraining structure, the conditioning structure is a social entity, in the sense that its goals conditioning is not necessarily attributable to any specific agent but is a general feature of the decision making system. Like the constraining structure, it is also objective, for its existence is an objective quality of the decision making system. Taken together these structures express the general (objective) asymmetries and (subjective) homogeneities in the decision making system. As the constraining structure signals the existence of objective forms of social coercion, the existence of a conditioning structure is a signal of the existence of subjective forms of social coercion.

Coercing mechanisms

When the constraining structure or the conditioning structure remains relatively stable in time, the problem arises of discovering the mechanisms that regulate its reproduction and evolution. In order to reproduce a general asymmetry or homogeneity in the decision making system, these mechanisms necessarily involve some general form of coercion. I shall call them 'coercive mechanisms'.

'Social coercion' is the combination of either a constraining or a conditioning structure and the mechanisms that reproduce it. Although, as we have seen, both these structures are objective, the resulting forms of social coercion can be classified as objective in the first case – when coercion operates via objective constraints – and subjective in the second, when it operates via subjective goals.

In both cases, social coercion is dynamic in nature. It does not reflect simply a general asymmetry and/or homogeneity in the decision making system in a point of time, but an asymmetry and/or homogeneity that is constantly reproduced over time. It can be grasped only by looking at the decision making system globally and dynamically.

Counter-mechanisms, counter-tendencies and counter-powers

Besides coercing mechanisms, there might exist other mechanisms that intervene in the reproduction of the constraining and the conditioning structures and that might either reinforce or contrast the action of existing coercing mechanisms. The existence of these mechanisms might be either independent from the general conditions of reproduction of the decision making system or an endogenous product of this process, a consequence of existing coercing mechanisms. Only in this second case, do these mechanisms assume scientific relevance and are an integral part of the ontology of power. Otherwise, they play the role of simple exogenous forces in the decision making system.

When these mechanisms develop as endogenous reactions against some coercing mechanisms, I shall call them 'counter-mechanisms'. Unlike coercing mechanisms, they are not a logical necessity in this ontology of power. Their concrete development is only a theoretical possibility created by the existence of coercive mechanisms. As reactions against other mechanisms, however, counter-mechanisms presuppose conscious action as well. They do not develop automatically.

The general effect of counter-mechanisms is to contrast the tendencies governed by coercing mechanisms, thereby generating 'counter-tendencies'. Concretely, this occurs through the generation of new forms of PTA and POS or through the transformation of pre-existing forms of power, which interact with the forms of power governed by coercing mechanisms. The concrete development of actual-empirical forms of power is regulated by the interaction of these tendencies and counter-tendencies.

This twofold opposition mechanisms/counter-mechanisms and tendencies/counter-tendencies does not necessarily produce an opposition between the forms of power that they govern. These oppositions regard, in fact, different ontological levels: causal mechanisms and tendencies are entities of the deep domain, PTAs and POSs occur in the actual-empirical domain. In principle, the forms of power governed by counter-mechanisms might either weaken or strengthen the constraining and the conditioning structures. To distinguish these forms of power, I shall call the former 'counter-powers'. Only these forms of power contrast the coercing role of the constraining and the conditioning structures. But counter-mechanisms might also govern forms of power that reinforce the constraining and conditioning structures.

Counter-powers in the actual-empirical domain are caused by counter-mechanisms in the deep domain, but their role as counter-powers is not a direct consequence of the opposition between coercing and counter-mechanisms in the deep domain. It is instead a consequence of the effects of this opposition in the actual-empirical domain: coercing mechanisms tend to reproduce the symmetries in the constraining structure and the homogeneities in the conditioning structure; counter-mechanisms tends instead to generate forms of power and counter-power, which might strengthen or weaken these asymmetries and homogeneities. To put it differently, counter-mechanisms and counter-tendencies are necessary but not sufficient conditions for the development of counter-powers.

Counter-powers do not simply attenuate the forms of social coercion in the decision making system, but constitute also an internal dynamic element in the decision making system, which might have either stabilising or destabilising effects: in some cases, counter-powers may facilitate the reproduction of the decision making system, in some other, they may act as potential causes of its instability and eventually lead to its crisis.

Systems of power

When we discuss a particular decision making system as a system of power, we do not mean simply that the PTAs (and the POSs that they eventually produce) are precisely defined. We mean something more, namely that a constraining or a conditioning structure and some coercing mechanisms (and eventually some counter-powers) exist as well. This is what makes a decision making system a 'system of power'.

A's PTA and goals can be influenced by completely different factors: in one case, they can be (partly) controlled by B via a direct relation of POS; in another case, they can be influenced by the tendencies caused by the coercing mechanisms that govern the evolution of the whole system of PTAs and goals, without any relation of POS. However, if the result is the same set of concrete decisions, then the difference between the two cases is only formal, not substantial.

This suggests that the analysis of power cannot be reduced to the study of POS, for if two agents are part of a system of power, their asymmetric PTAs and homogeneous preferences and interpretative frameworks can be systematically reproduced by impersonal structures and mechanisms without necessarily giving rise to relations of POS. This suggests also that, in a system of power, POS does not represent an essential form of power in the decision making system but is only a manifestation of the general forms of social coercion that govern the overall reproduction of PTAs and POSs.

This abstract definition of a system of power may apply to very different concrete contexts. It is basically a definition of social coercion in terms of the general structure of individual and interpersonal powers. It might characterise economic relation as well as gender or racial relations or any other sphere of social interaction characterised by social structures and reproducing mechanisms that constrain or condition agents' behaviour.

In no way, this general notion of social coercion depends directly on a notion of exploitation in the economy. Rather the opposite: the existence of social coercion opens the possibility that this social asymmetry produces also an economic result, as in the case of exploitation. But this is only a possibility, not a necessity. Social coercion, in other terms, is a necessary but not sufficient condition for exploitation. For instance, in capitalism, race relations or gender relations are strictly related to class relations and exploitation but have also an autonomous existence. The forms of power and coercion that these relations impose go well beyond the strict outcome of economic exploitation.

On the other hand, if we interpret this abstract ontology in the context of historical materialism, and we consider the conditions of reproduction of a mode of production, exploitation is not only a possibility but the essential driving force of social coercion. It is this economic relation that concretely shapes the forms of social coercion in each mode of production. Although, logically, the existence of exploitation depends on the existence of social coercion, in concrete historical developments, exploitation becomes the essential economic motive of social coercion.

But it is now time to move from a discussion of systems of power in general and consider the case of a specific mode of production, namely capitalism.

The ontology of capitalist power

Marx's *Capital* (1867, 1885, 1894) does not begin with the isolated individual, but with the commodity.[6] The commodity encapsulates all the distinguishing social relations of the capitalist mode of production. Material things are not in their nature commodities. They become commodities only under particular historical conditions, with particular social relations.

The category of the commodity itself encompasses the categories of private property and the market. Private property is a social relation that defines a series of duties and rights in society and their distribution among agents. The existence of private property thus implies the existence of power relations in the form of PTA.[7]

Through the market, commodities receive a social appraisal (the price system) and, on this basis, are exchanged. The exchange of commodities modifies the social system of duties and rights, i.e., modifies the system of individual PTAs. The coexistence of private property and the market gives rise to a specific form of PTA in the economy, namely, purchasing power: the power to buy. In barter, the parties exchange their respective PTAs over commodities directly. In monetary exchange, by contrast, one party alienates a concrete PTA (the power to dispose of a particular commodity) and receives money, i.e., the right to obtain commodities in the future. Money can thus be seen as an abstract PTA over commodities.

As we have seen, however, private property and the market are not sufficient to characterise capitalism. The specificity of capitalism is that the process of commodification includes labour power as well. In this case, the abstract form of PTA flowing from money takes also the form of POS relationship, a direct interpersonal power relation between of the buyer over the seller of labour power. More generally, the commodification of labour power transforms pre-existing modes of exploitation into capitalist exploitation. In this process, private property becomes capitalistic property – characterised by its individual variance and social invariance – and takes the form of a constraining structure between social classes.

This process transforms also pre-existing constraining and conditioning structures. With the development of the capitalist mode of production, capital tends to subsume the labour process and the whole society. The family, gender relations, race relations and other objective asymmetries existing in society are put under the governance of capital and its coercing mechanisms. These objective processes are also accompanied by transformations in subjective preferences and interpretative frameworks, which ultimately transform human nature itself.

In the materialist conception of history, these objective and subjective transformations are analysed as dialectically linked. Class relations, however, play a special role within all possible constraining and conditioning structures for their essential role in capitalistic exploitation. Unlike other social structures, class relations are a necessary feature of this mode of production. Other structures interact with this essential form of capitalist coercion and add other forms of coercion, not merely as independent processes, but rather as processes dialectically linked to the exploiting process. This is why they can be developed coherently only after the explanation of the essential form of social coercion that characterise capitalist exploitation.

Let me thus begin with purchasing power, as a form of PTA emanating from private property and the market, and then develop the main forms of POS and the non-observable structures and mechanisms that make capitalism a system of power.

Table 6.1 Capitalism as a system of power

Ontological domain	The ontology of power	The ontology of capitalist power
Actual-Empirical	Power to act	Purchasing power
	Power over somebody	Authority (production) Market power (circulation)
Deep	Constraining structures Conditioning structures Coercive mechanisms Counter-mechanisms	Class relations Superstructure Competition Association

Purchasing power

Purchasing power exists in all societies based on private property and the market. In capitalism, the central role of private property and the market makes purchasing power the essential form of PTA in the economy. It is determined by the distribution of property rights and the array of prices, which define the budget constraints of each agent. In general terms, the decision making set of an agent defines what the agent can and cannot *do*; in market relations, purchasing power defines what the agent can and cannot *buy*.

The quantitative differences between agents' purchasing power are a measure of the existing asymmetries of PTA in the economic sphere.[8] In capitalism, these quantitative asymmetries produce also a qualitative asymmetry: on one side, there are people that, given their (lack of) purchasing power, must *sell* their labour power; on the other side, other people, thanks to their purchasing power, can use it as capital and *buy* other people's labour power in order to make a profit from it.

In the economic debate on power, this general form of economic PTA is completely neglected. All authors focus directly on economic POS, without developing the relationship between these ontologically different forms of power. Bowles and Gintis (1994A, p. 301) are explicit on this issue: 'purchasing power in common parlance is not power at all in our usage, for the ability to acquire goods and services in a competitive economy in no way involves the use of sanctions'. In their view, this is only a bizarre terminological paradox – depending on their interest in POS, rather than in PTA – not a signal that their theory misses some essential aspect of capitalist economic coercion. The authors do not find any logical relation between these ontologically different entities (and their relations with the non-observable entities that govern both of them). In their theory of power, purchasing power and its asymmetric distribution in society simply play no essential role. Wealth might confers POS only to the extent that allocate agents to short side positions in non-clearing markets. This might occur, for instance, when financial markets are imperfect. But, as Bowles and Gintis (1990, p. 198) demonstrate 'Wealth ownership is neither necessary nor sufficient for holding short-side power'.

Authority and market power

POS takes different forms in production and in circulation: in production, it takes the form of authority relations; in circulation, that of market power.

Authority

Although the worker and the capitalist meet in the market on the basis of equal right (but with asymmetric purchasing power), the fact that one sells labour power and the other buys it produces a direct relation of POS between them in the process of production. This power relation in production is not caused by an unequal exchange in the sphere of circulation, but is rather the consequence of the exchange of this peculiar commodity, which involves human beings directly.

We have seen that the champions of the liberal view, Alchian and Demsetz, deny the existence of any real asymmetry between the worker and the capitalist on the ground that their interpersonal relation is like any other market relation. New institutionalists, like Coase, Williamson, Hart and Moore, have criticised this conception, by arguing that intra-firm relations are different from market relations, since the former involve formal authority and the latter are power-free. Bowles and Gintis have instead followed Alchian and Demsetz's idea the capitalist–worker relation is in fact a simple market relation but have shown that, under particular conditions, market relations might involve power. In a Marxist ontology of capitalism, these conceptions are all wrong and misleading.

When a grocer sells a kilo of coffee, he/she alienates a piece of his/her property and transfers to somebody else his/her power to do with the coffee as he/she likes. When a worker sells his/her labour power, he/she alienates a piece of his/her *life* and transfers to somebody else the power to do with *himself/herself* as he likes. The exchange of labour power, different from the exchange of other commodities, involves interpersonal relations directly. The PTA that the capitalist obtains in exchange for his money is itself a POS. He gives purchasing power to the worker and acquires authority over him/her. Clearly, the authority relationship is never absolute, since, like for any commodity, the utilisation of labour power is regulated by laws and institutional rules. However, within the existing norms, the economic POS involved in the exchange of the labour power is absolute, exactly as absolute is the economic PTA conferred by the ownership of any other commodity. The authority of the capitalist over the worker is not a theoretical possibility caused by the eventual existence of imperfections, but a necessary consequence of the inclusion of labour power in the reign of commodities, which characterises this mode of production.

This relation of POS in the workplace is probably the most visible manifestation of the social asymmetry between capitalists and workers. Its cause, however, is in this social asymmetry, which forces the worker to submit to a capitalist's authority, not in the interpersonal relation itself, as the post Walrasian method presupposes. Although intra-firm relations takes typically the form of authority, the social asymmetry between capitalists and workers is the true necessary condition that regulates the production process and the reproduction of wage labour. By contrast, its concrete manifestation in the form of one agent giving orders and another executing them, although typical of this mode of production, is not necessary at all, and occurs only when the capitalist and the worker do in fact enter a direct interpersonal relation. The authority relation is only the elementary mode of disciplining labour in capitalist production, but disciplining mechanisms are historically variable and do not necessarily give rise to such an open antagonism at an interpersonal level.

Consider, for instance, cooperative enterprises. Here, authority in the workplace is reduced or might even disappear. But this does not relax the general dependence of workers on capital and their subjugation to capital laws. The forms of power imposed on the worker by the class monopoly of the means of production become impersonal but do not cease to exist. Labour is no longer disciplined by a capitalist supervisor, like in the traditional capitalist firm, but by the dynamics of market prices, which imposes cooperatives' workers to self-organise, under capital laws, to pay capital its tribute. Formal authority is substituted by self-discipline under the direct guidance of the market coercing mechanism. Profit disappears formally, but – as a right to surplus value conferred by capital ownership – remains the essential motive of cooperative firms as well. 'This is why even workers' cooperatives producing commodities for the market will tend inevitably to "become their own capitalist" – they will be driven by market competition to accumulate a growing surplus from their own label in order to invest the new means of production which give them a fighting chance to meet the survival conditions established on the market' (McNally 1993, p. 181).

In capitalism, workers' self-organisation is not an abstract process but a process occurring under capital laws. Workers can do without the capitalist, but they need capital to start cooperative production. They might acquire it by means of a loan or the birth of the cooperative firm might be itself the initiative of a capitalist wishing to get rid of the annoying role of supervision. But, in a way or another, it will be workers' surplus value to remunerate anticipated capital.

Disciplining labour may be managed by personal or impersonal devices, but workers' exploitation remains the necessary condition for capitalist production also in this form of enterprise, apparently without authority. Concrete authority in the workplace is simply a manifestation of a social asymmetry, but the latter, not the former, is necessary to capitalist production. Interpersonal power-free relations during the labour process cannot cancel the essential coercive condition that makes all workers equal before capital: their freedom from the means of production.

Market power

In the sphere of circulation, an agent can influence the action of others only by having some control over the price system. Market power is thus the economic form of POS in circulation. It is defined as the power of the seller [buyer] to fix the price above [below] the price fixed by other sellers [buyers]. This form of economic power is not specific to capitalism; it is rather a potential feature of all systems based on private property and the market, for its existence presupposes market exchange, but not necessarily the market exchange of labour power. The specificity of capitalism is rather in the tendencies towards capital concentration and the consequent transformation of the prevailing market forms towards monopoly.

By considering authority and market power as economic forms of POS detached from the general structures and mechanisms of capitalism, they appear as merely theoretical possibilities, not as the empirical manifestations of the essential forms of coercion of this mode of production. This appearance is reinforced by the fact that there is no rigid empirical law in their concrete historical development since actual-empirical forms of power are 'out of phase' with the mechanisms that govern them. Only when these forms of power are put in relation with the necessary ontological entities of capitalism, they show their essential role in production and circulation. This role is a consequence of the general tendencies of capitalism, not of their particular empirical manifestations. Apparently, authority and market power are unnecessary both theoretically and empirically. Yet, they play an essential role as effects of the social structures and mechanisms that govern production and exchange in capitalism.

At a formal level, both authority and market power, as forms of economic POS, presuppose purchasing power, as a form of economic PTA. In order to have authority in production or market power in circulation, one must first have purchasing power, for the obvious reason that without the power to buy, one clearly cannot buy labour power, or any other commodity, at whatever price. The problem now is to explain how purchasing power on the one hand, and authority and market power on the other, are continuously transformed into one another and reproduced by the essential structures and mechanisms of this mode of production.

The class structure of capitalism

The constraining structure of capitalism is characterised by class relations. Class relations are not specific of capitalism but are a necessary condition for all modes of production characterised by exploitation. In capitalism, exploitation takes the form of a social relation between capital as a whole and the working class. This entails a form of social coercion, mostly indirect, operating through the asymmetric distribution of purchasing power in society, which brings a class of persons to work (voluntarily) for another class of persons.

In Marx's work, there is no systematic discussion of how to define social classes in capitalism.[9] The analysis of the capitalist mode of production in its pure form, developed in *Capital*, is based on a class structure with two main classes: capitalists and workers. In the study of concrete social formations (Marx 1847B, 1852, Marx and Engels 1848), however, Marx does not hesitate to consider a greater number of classes. This has prompted different interpretations of the theoretical status of classes in Marx's theory. According to an economistic interpretation, in *Capital*, classes are defined solely in terms of the economic structure, by the relation of each individual to the means of production, whilst in the analysis of concrete social formations classes must be defined also in terms of political and ideological structures. This interpretation, however, has been criticised for its strong separation of the economic structure, on the one hand, and political and ideological structures, on the other, as if the capitalist mode of production could effectively be defined in purely economic terms. Nicos Poulantzas (1973, ch. 2), in particular, argues that classes are the effect of the whole set of social structures that characterise the capitalist mode of production, and not solely of the economic structure.[10]

Here we do not need to develop these complex relations between the economic, the political and the ideological structures of capitalism. The economic separation of the population into buyers and sellers of labour power is sufficient to determine an essential aspect of class relations in capitalism. This is not to reduce social classes to an asymmetry in economic constraints; it is rather to recognise that the asymmetric distribution of purchasing power is an essential aspect of every definition of the class structure of capitalism.

With these caveats, capitalist class structure can be characterised by capitalists' monopoly of the means of production. Abstractly, private property and the market might exist without class divisions. Class monopoly of the means of production, however, is the necessary condition for the development of wage labour and for the functioning of capitalism. Without such an asymmetry between buyers and sellers of labour power, no stable labour market would exist. The asymmetric distribution of purchasing power in society is thus not only a theoretical possibility, but a necessary condition for the reproduction of the system. Notwithstanding the never-ending dreams of the bourgeois economist attached to egalitarianism, with a really symmetrical distribution of purchasing power in society, capitalist production would not even begin.

Considered from the viewpoint of constraints, wage labour exists only as long as a class of people is *constrained* to sell labour power. The other side of the coin is that another class of people is *enabled* to buy labour power. This is the essential asymmetry of the capitalist constraining structure (which capitalists might well call it an 'enabling structure'): workers are constrained by their lack of purchasing power; capitalists are enabled by their possession of it.

The economic result of this social asymmetry is class exploitation. The specificity of exploitation in capitalism is that it is not necessarily realised through direct relations of POS but is realised through the social shaping of PTAs into a constraining structure.

The feudal lord gets part of the product of his serf (and much more) thanks to his direct power relation over him/her. The relation of POS between them is the vehicle through which exploitation imposes its coercing rules in the feudal society. The value appropriated by the capitalist is instead only a function of the general exploitation of his class over the working class, but is not directly linked to his power relation over his own worker. Their relation of POS is not the direct vehicle through which exploitation imposes its rules in the capitalist society and the proof is that it may even disappear concretely, like in cooperative enterprises. Unlike feudalism, here exploitation imposes its rules via the constraining structure, not via relations of POS.

The capitalist superstructure

According to Marx's historical materialism, individuals are free to act within the existing social context, but are conditioned in their very consciousness by the mode of production of their material life (Marx 1859, preface; Marx and Engels 1845, Part 1). This means that subjective preferences and interpretative frameworks, like objective constraints, are influenced by the forms of social interaction. Within historical materialism, these objective and subjective processes are analysed as parts of a dialectical relation between the base and the superstructure of capitalism.[11]

The role of superstructural powers and their relation with the forms of social coercion emanating from the base are developed, in particular, by Gramsci (1929–35). In his critique, the revolutionary leader discusses both the class nature of culture, education and ideology and their role in the reproduction and evolution of class relations. He shows that this dialectical relation is not at all mechanic or predetermined but, on the contrary, is part of an open process, in which self-reinforcing coercive tendencies can be contrasted concretely by the development of forms of counter-power, practices of social struggle and processes of social emancipation. In his political strategy, he insists on the role of the superstructure to force transformations in the base as well. The struggles in the cultural, political and ideological spheres are an integral part of a general subversive strategy against capitalism. But it is clear that if these struggles do not produce effects also in the economic sphere, their revolutionary role will remain limited and ineffective.

Unsurprisingly, this dialectical conception has had no impact on the economic debate on power. But even within Marxism, Gramsci's contribution has not always been developed accurately and has sometimes led to over-emphasise the superstructure and downplay its dialectics with the base.

In a Marxist-Gramscian conception, the logical relation with exploitation is the key to define the essential or inessential forms of (structural and superstructural) power in the capitalist mode of production. It is not an a-priori assumption about the mechanical dominance of the base over the superstructure, as some Marx's critics maintain, but the result of an ontological enquiry into the coercing forces of this mode of production.

Theoretically, a system of power may reproduce itself even by reproducing only its conditioning structure, without any constraining structure. For instance, morality, religion or culture may, in fact, impose sufficient conditionings on agents' subjective preferences and interpretative frameworks, so to lead them towards choices and behaviours that reproduce the asymmetries and homogeneities existing in society. The development of these systems of (superstructural) power, however, is not a direct consequence of capitalist exploitation. Therefore, when they actually develop in capitalism, they coexist necessarily with the forms of coercion that regulate the exploitative process. Even if they pre-existed capitalism, their own development gets thus transformed under the laws of capital. Like other social relations, they are subsumed under capital. In concrete capitalist systems, they may play an important coercive role, but this role can be properly understood only by considering their interaction with the specific forms of coercion of capitalism. As purely autonomous forces, by contrast, they are not necessary at all in this mode of production.

Consider morality. Although it might appear as a set of 'permanent principles which stand above history and the differences between nations, ... all moral theories have been hitherto the product, in the last analysis, of the economic conditions of society obtaining at the time. And as society has hitherto moved in class antagonisms, morality has always been class morality' (Engels 1877, ch. 9). In capitalism, the affirmation of bourgeois morality is a consequence of the economic dominion of the capitalist class over the proletariat. Although moral systems have their own reproducing mechanisms, these mechanisms get transformed when they enter in contact with the mechanism of reproduction of class relations. A dominant morality does not emerge simply as a consequence of the moral strength of its beliefs and precepts, but is to a large extent the consequence of the same economic mechanisms that reproduce asymmetrical class relations and impose the morality of the ruling class on the whole society. This is why even in the analysis of subjective powers and conditioning structures, we must discuss their relation with the forms of social coercion conveyed by the constraining structure.

Competition

The main mechanism that regulates the reproduction of class relations in capitalism is 'competition'. Competition is born with the market, but becomes the specific reproducing mechanism of capitalism only with the birth of the *labour* market. To put it differently, the existence of competition is a consequence of private property and alienated labour, but it is only with the full development of capital that it becomes the general coordinating and coercing mechanism of this mode of production.

The development of capital and the development of competition describe in fact the same process, seen from the angle of capital as a whole and from that of the relations between individual capitals. Historically, this process has not created exploitation but has rather transformed pre-existing class societies and their modes of exploitation, by placing them in a capitalist framework regulated by competition.

With the development of capitalism, competition becomes the means by which capital subsumes the whole society. Its action is not limited to the economic sphere but tends to develop in all forms of social interactions, even in the reproduction of culture, moral systems, politics and religions.

As the vehicle of the process of subsumption of society under capital, competition transforms also the values and norms that guide the reproduction of subjective preferences and interpretative frameworks, by impressing its class nature on them. Competition is thus internalised subjectively and becomes the very human nature of this mode of production.

In the reproduction of the constraining structure of capitalism, competition operates as the invisible hand of capital. It regulates the relations between individual capitals by enforcing the general laws of capital. Logically, these laws – which include exploitation – exist before competition. Competition simply enforces them in the concrete process of capital accumulation, by guiding individual action along the process of capitalist exploitation. The scientific problem is that these laws are invisible in the reign of competition and, as we have seen, can be discovered only by an analysis of capital as a whole.

In bourgeois economics, competition is generally conceived of as a state of affairs (neoclassical competition, with large numbers and small dimensions) or as a process (Austrian conception of the market as a discovery procedure). However, as in the case of power, these conceptions only confuse the mechanisms that govern actual-empirical phenomena with the phenomena themselves. In a stratified ontology, which separates the actual-empirical from the deep domain, competition is better understood as a causal mechanism.

In general terms, 'competition is the completest expression of the battle of all against all'. In a class society, however, this battle 'is fought not between the different classes of society only, but also between the individual members of these classes' (Engels 1845, ch. 3). The dialectical relation between these two battles is the concrete way in which competition governs the reproduction of class relations and give them the form of a constraining structure. Consider first the battle *between* classes. In this battle, like in any other, the stronger often wins. And it is not difficult to understand that workers and capitalists have not the same strength, for the former must work to live, whilst the latter can live on their capital. The asymmetric strength between classes influences competition *within* classes as well: competition tends to be stronger within the weaker class, i.e. on the workers' side. This asymmetry, in turn, reinforces the asymmetric strength *between* classes, since the stronger the competition within one class, the weaker the whole class in its relation to the other.

This asymmetric competition between and within classes regulates wage dynamics and unemployment. It pushes the wage towards the subsistence level and creates a structural surplus population with respect to the needs of capital valorisation, the so-called 'industrial reserve army of labour' (Marx 1867, chap 22). These tendencies prevent concretely workers from becoming independent from wage labour. Although individual social mobility is not precluded, the social effect of these myriads of individual stories is socially constrained. As a whole, these individual processes must in fact constantly reproduce a class of propertyless persons, constrained by their insufficient purchasing power to sell their labour power. This is the essential form of social coercion that keeps the exploitative process in motion.

These tendencies of capital accumulation and the consequent forms of social coercion have nothing to do with eventual imperfections in the working of competition. They are rather intrinsic structural consequences of its normal working. In neoclassical models, clearing markets may be assumed everywhere. In real capitalism, however, the labour market never clears. Neoclassical economists may search the cause of this phenomenon in the lack of competition. But in real capitalism it is precisely competition that causes it.

Association

'Association' is as old as social life. It plays different roles in different modes of production and exists since the first forms of primitive communism. With the development of capitalism and the rise of competition as its general coercing mechanism, however, its economic role changes. Association gets transformed by competition and develops as a reaction against it, as a counter-mechanism. It takes the form of a visible hand, governed by a piece of society, against the invisible hand of capital, which divides society into isolated individuals – a conscious collective action against the impersonal mechanism of competition.

Like competition, this conscious (re)action develops within class relations and, with the development of the capitalist mode of production, becomes itself a class mechanism, operating both between and within classes.

In the relations between classes, association contrasts competition and tends to produce associative forms in which class conflicts and the asymmetric strength of each class are integrated within the association. Corporations and other institutional forms finalised to recompose the conflicting interests between classes are concrete examples of interclass association. Of course, this mode of managing the conflicting interests between classes is not the end of conflicting interests, but only a way to let them develop without any open battle between classes. But, by definition, in a class system, there is no way to truly and fully harmonise the material interests of the opposing social classes. Interclass association simply suffocates class struggle and the explosion of overt class conflicts, by internalising the structural asymmetry existing between classes within the associative form. Therefore, notwithstanding the appearance of a symmetrical role of all participants, interclass associations are structurally asymmetrical in terms of their internal power relations.

Association contrasts competition within classes as well. Within both classes, it leads the members of the same class to ally and cooperate to counter the effects of competition among themselves. Like in the case of interclass association, its social effect is to unite what competition separates. Here however association regards the members of the same class, rather than the members of opposing classes. The class asymmetry in the constraining and the conditioning structures produces here an asymmetry in the way association develops within each class. Association is easier and, in a sense, spontaneous on the dominant side of class relations, whereas it encounters more obstacles on the dominated side, in which intra-class competition is a greater obstacle to association.

On the side of capitalists, association leads to the formation of formal organisations or informal agreements, whose general effect is to strengthen the capitalist class in its relation with the working class. This tendency reinforces the asymmetric effect of competition on class relations. Association between capitalists and competition work in the same direction, as expressions of the dominion of capital over labour.

Association between workers tends instead to blunt the sharpest weapon of the bourgeoisie and to weaken the coercing role of competition on the working class. Here association and competition work in opposite direction from the viewpoint of class asymmetries. Through trade unions, political associations and class struggle, workers can overtly fight against the constraining structure of this mode of production and improve their general relation with capital. In this sense, these forms of collective power are better understood as 'counter-powers'.

This juxtaposition between powers and counter-powers is not a consequence of the opposition between competition and association as such. It rather regards the way competition and association interact with the constraining structure. Competition, as the mechanism that enforces capital exploitation, enforces also the social coercion of capital. Concretely, it does it by regulating the reproduction of the constraining and the conditioning structures. Association, by contrast, in its reaction against competition, produces forms of collective PTA, which may strengthen or weaken the constraining and the conditioning structures. Only in this sense, can we characterise these forms of PTA emanating from association as powers or counter-powers.

Unlike competition, association is not really necessary for the development of capitalism. It may materialise on one side of the capital–labour relationship, on both sides or on neither of them, but capitalism goes on anyway. Indeed the *Wal-Mart* model of capitalism without trade unions is not only possible, but also very profitable.

By counteracting competition, association can have both stabilising or destabilising effects on the reproduction of the system. Consider, for instance, the effects of workers' association. By opposing the tendency of competition to 'over-exploit' labour power, association acts as a stabilising force, which helps the reproduction of labour power and the perpetuation of the process of exploitation. By contrasting the maximum extraction of living labour from labour power, however, it tends to compress the rate of exploitation and reinforces therefore the tendency of the profit rate to fall.

But, as we have seen, association is also the mechanism that allows fighting frontally against this system of power, it is the pre-condition for all revolutionary movements. It is both the means to contrast the coercing mechanism of competition in capitalism and the goal of a new society, without exploitation, its enforcing mechanism and its associated forms of social coercion.

The capitalist system of power

The class structure of capitalism and the coercive mechanism of competition make capitalism a system of power. Within this system, the distributions of PTA and POS are constantly reproduced, under the rules of competition. These rules are the means by which capital imposes the forms of social coercion necessary to carry out the process of exploitation.

This form of social coercion is an essential aspect of the capitalist ontology of power. It is objective and its existence does not depend on its concrete detection by some agents of the opposing classes. On the contrary, it is empirically invisible and detectable only by means of scientific investigation. The reason of its invisibility is competition. The latter tends in fact to separate individuals and make them appear as independent from each other. It tends thus to mask their social role and gives a coercive social relation the appearance of a free interpersonal relation.

The counter-mechanism of this system of power is association. Different from competition, this mechanism operates by producing visible forms of collective PTAs. The paradox is that these counter-powers – which are not even essential entities in this ontology – appear as the very sources of power, once the coercive role of competition has become invisible. Rather than counter-powers developing as reaction against capitalist structural coercion, in bourgeois economics, these PTAs appear as the cause of power in a system of power-free relations. In this mystified conception, trade unions are not tools to defend workers in their struggle to reduce capital coercion. They are rather an imperfection to the perfectly competitive model, whose consequences are unemployment, employment rents and power relations.

In the concrete development of the capitalist mode of production, the essential forms of social coercion tend to coexist with other forms of power and coercion, which are not essential for the capitalist system of power. Race relations, gender relations, politics, religion and other objective or subjective social divisions may add new forms of power and coercion to the essential coercive forces of capitalism. In this process, however, they do not act independent on class relations, but are reshaped by them (and contribute to shape them). This is why a study of these systems of power, which abstracts from the essential coercion of the capitalist mode of production, might be deeply misleading.

Let me give a rough example. In theoretical schemes based on gender or racial relations, abstracting from class relations, the premiership of Thatcher in the United kingdom or the presidency of Barack Obama in the United states – the first woman and the first black to have reached these positions – may appear as advancements towards egalitarianism and real democracy. If however class relations are taken into account, it is dubious that their climb to the top of the UK and US political power has reduced the subordinated role of British female and North-American black workers, who continue to suffer their twofold oppression, as workers and as women or blacks. Perhaps, gender and race relations played some role in their political career, in the name of abstract anti-sexist and anti-racist principles, but this only confirms that, in capitalism, these social divisions are secondary and inessential with respect to class relations. From the viewpoint of social classes, any worker knows that Mrs. Thatcher and Mr. Obama are not at all expressions of counter-powers generated by the exploited and dominated parts of society, but rather exponents of the ruling class, actively involved in class struggle against workers, male and female, black and white.[12]

Politically, this methodological approach to power, which does not consider the essential forms of coercion of capitalism, lay itself open to all sorts of opportunism. 'Positive discrimination' opens the doors of power position to well-educated women and exponents of the black bourgeoisie, but does not improve – and might even worsen – the objective conditions of female and black workers. The petty-bourgeois philosopher may insist that the premiership of a woman and the presidency of a black are decisive democratising steps, but the feminist movement and the *Black Panther Party*, not Mrs. Thatcher and Mr. Obama, will be remembered for the conquest of British women rights and for the black people self-defence in the United states.

Conclusions

Economic power takes different forms in capitalism. Neoclassical economics, however, considers only the surface of interpersonal relations, in which power relations manifest themselves in the form of POS. This restriction occurs without any systematic analysis of the relations between POS and PTA and without any investigation on the factors that govern the evolution of the distribution of PTA in society. The cause of this, I have argued, lies in the empirical realist ontology that underlies neoclassical economics.

Against this conception, I have drawn upon critical realism to develop a sophisticated ontology of power relations under capitalism, an ontology in which empirical and observable forms of power are put in relation to the structures and mechanisms that govern them. In line with Marx's method and analysis, I have shown that capitalism is a system of power, in which the forms of POS (market power and authority) depend on the distribution of PTA (purchasing power) in society. These phenomenal forms of power are the manifestations of the existing relations of social coercion caused by the constraining structure (characterised by class relations) and the coercing mechanism that reproduces it (competition). In addition to these essential forms of power and coercion, I have argued that capitalism is characterised by other forms of power and coercion emanating from its conditioning structures (superstructural powers). And I have suggested that all forms of power governed by the coercing mechanism of competition can be contrasted and eventually abolished by the development of its counter-mechanism (association).

This ontological investigation shows the limits of the mystifying conception of mainstream economics of capitalism as being possibly free from power relations. The problem is not simply that Walrasian competition does not exist in reality, but rather that such a hypothetical system could not work and reproduce itself without forms of social coercion governed by structures and mechanisms that are not necessarily detectable empirically. The ontology of mainstream economics cannot consider these forms of social coercion because, more generally, it does not allow the distinction between appearances and essence, between formal and substantial power relations. If capitalist relations are power relations, however, it is not because they necessarily appear as such empirically, but because capitalism is in its essence a system of power.

Notes

1 Within neoclassical economics, the most organic attempt to conceptualise power by means of decision theory is developed by Bartlett (1989). The author's goal is to facilitate formal inclusion of power in neoclassical modelling. As a

consequence, he remains attached to an interpersonal conception of power and develops it within the flat neoclassical ontology, in which there is no room for social coercion.

2   This explains why Austrian economics, the champion of methodological individualism, but also a severe critic of neoclassical *homo economicus*, has never really participated to the debate on power within mainstream economics.

3   In a review of Lawson's 2003 book *Reorienting Economics*, Pinkstone (2003) criticises the author for defining economics in terms of social relations, but without any specific reference to power. He argues that neoclassical economists do not deny that capitalists and workers are engaged in a social relationship, but maintain that this relationship does not necessarily involve power. Pinkstone suggests that Marx is the economist who made social power the central focus of his explanation of production and distribution in capitalism. What follows can be seen as an attempt to follow Lawson's reorientation of economics by taking account of Pinkstone's criticism.

4   Within methodological individualism, Austrian economics develops this difference between information and knowledge but, at the same time, rejects, by assumption, any external influence on individual's interpretative frameworks, which, like preferences, are assumed to be inborn individual qualities.

5   This definition of authority is inspired by the notion elaborated by Marx and Engels: 'the imposition of the will of another upon ours' (Engels 1872). It is also compatible with the definition of neoclassical economics, although, within this literature, the notion of authority is also referred to as 'hierarchy', 'verticality', or 'command'. In political writings, the term authority is sometimes used to describe situations in which '*B* complies because he recognises that *A*'s command is reasonable in terms of his own values' (Bachrach and Baratz 1970, p. 34). This latter meaning takes inspiration from Weber's (1968) conception of 'legitimate authority' that presupposes a consent to obey commands. Unlike my definition, which is purely objective, this notion of authority is based on the subjective elements of the decision making process.

6   Mattick (1993) maintains that *Capital* begins with the commodity only because Marx intended to criticise classical political economy (which often starts with the commodity), but the real theoretical starting point is class relations. This interpretation contrasts the logical-historical interpretation of Marx's categories suggested by Engels (1886) and developed by Meek (1976), according to which the structure of *Capital* reflects an idealised periodisation of history from pre-capitalist 'simple commodity production' to proper capitalist production. Earlier critiques of this interpretation are developed by Banaji (1979) and Smith (1990). For an analysis of the significance of the opening chapters of *Capital*, see Pilling (1980, ch. 4).

7   Outside of Marxism, the economic coercion emanating from property is investigated in particular by institutionalist authors, such as Veblen (1934), Samuels (1979 ed., 1984, 1994) and Schmid (1987). The relations between Marxism and institutionalism in the analysis of power and classes are discussed by Klein (1992) and Dugger and Sherman (1994).

8   Within the institutionalist tradition, Schutz (1995) discusses the asymmetric distribution of purchasing power as a potential cause of relations of POS in the market. The author, however, does not develop any analysis of this asymmetry as an essential aspect of the capitalist economic structure.

9 In the third volume of *Capital*, there is a draft chapter dedicated to the subject. However, the chapter is incomplete and its purpose seems to be more to point out the problematic aspects of defining classes, than to provide the blueprints for such a project.

10 Cf. also Poulantzas (1986). Colletti (1972) criticises Kautsky's and Plekhanov's orthodoxy and Bernstein's revisionism for their separation of the economic structure from the other social structures of capitalism, and argues that Marx's 'economic sphere' in fact embraces the production of things as well as ideas, and material production as well as the production of social relations. In developing Colletti's interpretation, Sayer (1987) maintains that the attempt to separate forces and relations of production, or base and superstructure, as if they referred to different bits of empirical reality, presupposes an atomistic ontology that is extraneous to Marx's.

11 Outside of Marxism, the institutional school in particular has studied the mechanisms through which power relations concur to shape individuals' goals and interpretative frameworks. Galbraith (1983) analyses three forms of power: 'condign' (power is a consequence of a threat), 'compensatory' (power is acquired by means of a reward) and 'conditioned' (power is exercised by changing individuals beliefs). The first two operate within given preferences and interpretative frameworks, the third transforms these subjective elements as well. Dugger (1984, 1989) focuses on the process through which corporations impose their values and culture in society. Outside of economic debates, this issue is illustrated with rich empirical evidence by Klein (2000).

12 A lucid example of how to develop racial relations in a class framework, inspired to Marx and Gramsci, is developed by Wilson's (2011). He criticises progressive scholars who have analysed racial oppression by detaching it from economic exploitation and discusses the historical development of racism in the US as part of the transformations in class relations.

References

Archer, Margaret (1995), *Realist social theory: The morphogenetic approach*, Cambridge, Cambridge University Press.

Archer, Margaret, Roy Bhaskar, Andrew Collier, Tony Lawson and Alan Norrie (1988 eds), *Critical realism: Essential readings*, London, Routledge.

Bachrach, Peter and Morton Baratz (1970), *Power and poverty. Theory and practice*, New York, Oxford University Press.

Banaji, Jarius (1979), From the commodity to capital: Hegel's dialectic in Marx's *Capital*, in Elson, Diane (ed.), *Value: The representation of labor in capitalism*, London, CSE Books.

Bartlett, Randall (1989), *Economics and power: An inquiry into human relations and markets*, Cambridge, Cambridge University Press.

Bhaskar, Roy (1978), *A realist theory of science*, Hemel Hempstead, Harvester Press.

——(1979), *The possibility of naturalism*, Hemel Hempstead, Harvester Press.

——(1991), *Philosophy and the idea of freedom*, Oxford, Blackwell.

——(1986), *Scientific realism and human emancipation*, London, Verso.

——(1993), *Dialectic: The pulse of freedom*, London, Verso.

Bowles, Samuels and Herbert Gintis (1990), Contested exchange: New microfoundations for the political economy of capitalism, *Politics and Society*, vol. 18, n. 2, pp. 165–222.

——(1994A), Power in economic theory, in Philip Arestis and Malcolm Sawyer (eds), *The Elgar companion to radical political economy*, Aldershot, Edward Elgar.

Brown, Andrew, Steve Fleetwood and Michael Roberts (2001), The marriage of critical realism and Marxism: Happy, unhappy or on the rocks?, in Brown, Andrew, Steve Fleetwood and Michael Roberts (eds), *Critical realism and Marxism*, London, Routledge.

Colletti, Lucio (1972), Bernstein and the Marxism of the second international, in Colletti, Lucio (ed.), *From Rousseau to Lenin*, London, New Left Books.

Collier, Andrew (1979), Materialism and explanation in the human sciences, in Mepham, John and David-Hillel Ruben (eds), *Issues in Marxist philosophy*, Brighton, The Harvester Press.

——(1989), *Scientific realism and socialist thought*, Hemel Hempstead, Harvester Wheatsheaf.

——(1994), *Critical realism: An introduction to Roy Bhaskar's philosophy*, London, Verso.

Creaven, Sean (2001), *Marxism and realism: A materialistic application of realism in the social sciences*, London, Routledge.

——(2003), Marx and Bhaskar on the dialectics of freedom, *Journal of Critical Realism*, vol. 2, n. 1, pp. 63–93.

Dugger, William (1984), *An alternative to economic retrenchment*, New York, Petrocelli Books.

——(1989), *Corporate power*, New York, Greenwood Press.

Dugger, William and Howard Sherman (1994), A comparison of Marxism and institutionalism, *Journal of Economic Issues*, vol. 28, n. 1, pp. 101–27.

Ehrbar, Hans (1998). *Marxism and critical realism*, University of Utah. Retrieved from www.criticalrealism.com/archive/hehrbar_mcr.pdf (accessed 1 March 2016).

——(2001), Critical realist argument in Marx's *Capital*, in Brown, Andrew, Steve Fleetwood and Michael Roberts (eds), *Critical realism and Marxism*, London, Routledge.

Engels, Frederick (1845), The *conditions of the working-class in England*. Retrieved from www.marxists.org/archive/marx/works/1845/condition-working-class/index.htm (accessed 1 March 2016).

——(1872), *On authority*. Retrieved from www.marxists.org/archive/marx/works/1872/10/authority.htm (accessed 1 March 2016).

——(1877), *Anti-Dühring. Herr Eugen Dühring's revolution in science*. Retrieved from www.marxists.org/archive/marx/works/1877/anti-duhring (accessed 1 March 2016).

——(1886), *Ludwig Feuerbach and the end of classical German philosophy*. Retrieved from www.marxists.org/archive/marx/works/1886/ludwig-feuerbach/index.htm (accessed 1 March 2016).

Fleetwood, Steve (1999 ed.), *Critical realism in economics: Development and debate*, London, Routledge.

Galbraith, John (1983), *The anatomy of power*, Boston, Houghton Mifflin.

Gramsci, Antonio (1929–35), *Prison notebooks*. Retrieved from www.marxists.org/archive/gramsci/prison_notebooks/index.htm (accessed 1 March 2016).

Gunn, Richard (1989), Marxism and philosophy: A critique of critical realism, *Capital and Class*, vol. 37, pp. 86–116.

Joseph, Jonathan (2001), Five ways in which critical realism can help Marxism, in Brown, Andrew, Steve Fleetwood and Michael Roberts (eds), *Critical realism and Marxism*, London, Routledge.

Klein, Naomi (2000), *No Logo*, Toronto, Alfred A. Knopf.

Klein, Philip (1992), Institutionalists, radical economists, and class, *Journal of Economic Issues*, vol. 26, n. 2, pp. 535–44.

Lawson, Tony (1997). *Economics and reality*, London, Routledge.

——(2003), *Reorienting economics*, London, Routledge.

Magill, Kevin (1994), Against critical realism, *Capital and Class*, vol. 54, pp. 113–36.

Marx, Karl (1847B), *The poverty of philosophy*. Retrieved from www.marxists.org/archive/marx/works/1847/poverty-philosophy/index.htm (accessed 1 March 2016).

——(1852), *The 18th brumaire of Louis Napoleon*. Retrieved from www.marxists.org/archive/marx/works/1852/18th-brumaire/ (accessed 1 March 2016).

——(1859), *A contribution to the critique of political economy*. Retrieved from www.marxists.org/archive/marx/works/1859/critique-pol-economy (accessed 1 March 2016).

——(1867), *Capital: Critique of political economy, vol, 1, The process of capitalist production*. Retrieved from www.marxists.org/archive/marx/works/1867-c1/index.htm (accessed 1 March 2016).

——(1885), *Capital: Critique of political economy, vol, 2, The process of circulation of capital*. Retrieved from www.marxists.org/archive/marx/works/1885-c2/index.htm (accessed 1 March 2016).

——(1894), *Capital: Critique of political economy, vol, 3, The process of capitalist production as a whole*. Retrieved from www.marxists.org/archive/marx/works/1894-c3/index.htm (accessed 1 March 2016).

Marx, Karl and Frederick Engels (1845), The German ideology. Retrieved from www.marxists.org/archive/marx/works/1845/german-ideology/index.htm (accessed 1 March 2016).

——(1848), *The communist manifesto*. Retrieved from www.marxists.org/archive/marx/works/1848/communist-manifesto/index.htm (accessed 1 March 2016).

Mattick, Paul Jr (1993), Marx's dialectic, in Moseley, Fred (ed.), *Marx's method in Capital: A reexamination*, Atlantic Highlands, Humanities Press.

McNally, David (1993), *Against the market: Political economy, market socialism and the Marxist critique*, London, Verso.

Meek, Ronald (1976), *Studies in the labor theory of value*, New York, Monthly Review Press.

Norris, Christopher (1999), Roy Bhaskar interviewed, *The Philosopher's Magazine*, vol. 8.

Outhwaite, William (1987), *New philosophies of social science: Realism, hermeneutics and critical theory*, London, Macmillan.

Pilling, Geoff (1980), *Marx's Capital, philosophy and political economy.* Retrieved from www.marxists.org/archive/pilling/works/capital/index.htm (accessed 1 March 2016).

Pinkstone, Brian (2003), Reorienting economics: New horizons, Review of 'Reorienting economics' by Tony Lawson, *Journal of Critical Realism*, vol. 2, n. 1, pp. 149–55.

Poulantzas, Nicos (1973), *Political power and social classes*, London, Verso.

——(1986), Class power, in Lukes, Steven (ed.), *Power*, Oxford, Basil Blackwell.

Roberts, John (1999), Marxism and critical realism, *Capital and Class*, vol. 68, pp. 21–49.

Samuels, Warren (1979 ed.), *The economy as a system of power*, New Jersey, Transaction Books.

——(1984), On the nature and existence of economic coercion: The correspondence of Robert Lee Hale and Thomas Nixon Carver, *Journal of Economic Issues*, vol. 18, n. 4, pp. 1027–48.

——(1994), Property, in Hodgson, Geoffrey, Warren Samuels and Marc Tool (eds), *The Elgar companion to institutional and evolutionary economics*, Aldershot, Edward Elgar.

Sayer, Derek (1987), *The violence of abstraction*, Oxford, Basil Blackwell.

Schmid, Allan (1987), *Property, power, and public choice: An inquiry into law and economics*, New York, Praeger.

Schutz, Eric (1995), Markets and power, *Journal of Economic Issues*, vol. 29, n. 4, pp. 1147–70.

Smith, Tony (1990), The debate regarding dialectic logic in Marx's economic writings, *International Philosophical Quarterly*, vol. 30, n. 3, pp. 289–98.

Veblen, Throstein (1934), The beginnings of ownership, in Ardzrooni, Leon (ed.), *Essays in our changing order*, New York, The Viking Press.

Weber, Max (1968), *Economy and society*, New York, Bedminster Press.

Wilson, Carter (2011), The dominant class and the construction of racial oppression: A neo-Marxist/Gramscian approach to race in the United States, vol. 25, n. 1. Retrieved from http://sdonline.org/55/the-dominant-class-and-the-construction-of-racial-oppression-a-neo-marxistgramscian-approach-to-race-in-the-united-states (accessed 1 March 2016).

7 Final remarks

In his contribution for the *Journal of economic perspectives*, titled 'Post Walrasian and post Marxian economics', Stiglitz (1993) discusses explicitly the relations between the radical approach and the mainstream developments of Walrasian economics, based on imperfections and transaction costs. He argues that there are striking parallels between these approaches, that they use the same method and set of assumptions and that they deal basically with the same problem. The difference, in his view, is only about terminology: 'Mainstream economists have not only found concepts like exploitation and power to be useless in explaining economic phenomena, but they worry about introducing such emotionally charged words into the analysis. But that is presumably precisely why the radical economists choose to use such words: they want the analysis to motivate action' (Stiglitz 1993, p. 112).

It is not very surprising that the winner of the Nobel Prize considers exploitation and power as 'emotionally charged words', rather than scientific categories, and that, by contrast, he considers efficiency – the key word of the neoliberal political program – as a value-free notion.[1] But this is only a confirmation that value judgements are easily detectable only when they break the beliefs that form the cultural hegemony of each time. Otherwise they may appear as neutral, even though the very possibility of pure objectivity in social research is a very controversial issue.[2]

Apart from this consideration, I share fully Stiglitz's conclusion about the mutual consistency of these approaches within the post Walrasian research program. This is, however, only half of the story. The second half regards the relation with Marx. In this book, I have thus explicitly espoused a Marxist perspective and I have submitted to critique the theory, the method, the ontology and the ideology of post Walrasian economics.

I have shown that Marx and post Walrasian economists follow radically different methods. One starts with the commodity, within a historical system based on commodity production; the others start with the individual, within an abstract system of complete and perfect markets. One develops his critique dialectically, by analysing the logical and historical development of the essential categories of the capitalist mode of production; the others operate deductively, by means of comparative statics exercises, which describe processes that logically and historically have nothing to do with the development of capitalism. I have argued that these methodological choices presuppose different economic ontologies: a stratified one, in one case, with a logical separation between the empirical forms of power and the non-observable structures and mechanisms that govern them; and a flat, purely empirical, one, in the other, with power and competition sharing the spectrum of economic relations according to the presence/absence of imperfections in the DMC. And I have concluded that, paradoxically, competition – the negation of power, according to post Walrasians – is the very coercive mechanism of capitalism, according to Marx.

Let me now draw some general conclusions from my critique. First, I wish to question the very *raison d'être* of post Walrasian radicalism, by discussing the narrow and purely formal sense in which it can substantiate the Marxist central antagonism between capitalists and workers. This issue is not purely academical. To be incapable, or unwilling, to develop Marx's conception is not a capital sin. But having missed the scientific mission of an epoch is a more serious blame. In a period in which social movements were uprising against all forms of power and coercion, radical post Walrasians have developed a conception in which power is a simple interpersonal relation, which develops naturally, for personal convenience. Some of them have been rewarded with prestige and academic power for their theoretical contributions. But only by other academicians, not by people struggling against capital chains. This is the second implication of post Walrasian economics that I wish to develop: willy-nilly, this approach has increased, not reduced, the gap between economic theory and social struggles. Today, this gap is one of the main theoretical obstacles in the definition of an organic and unitary strategy within the anti-capitalist movement. Therefore, to conclude, I try to suggest how the conception of capitalism as a system of power might reorient scientific research and the political struggle.

Formal similarities within opposite conceptions

Marx

The main theoretical problem in the attempt to explain the working of capitalism and its forms of coercion is that this mode of production is mystified. Indeed, one of the specificities of capitalism is that its exploitative nature is hidden behind the appearance of competition. Therefore, Marx's critique of political economy is not a simple reply to his theoretical and political rivals. It is rather a way to demystify the appearances of capitalist reality – which bourgeois economists rationalise – and explain scientifically the mechanisms that govern this mode of production and that tend to produce these mystified appearances. The complexity of Marx's critique stems from this twofold scientific goal: discovering the hidden exploitative and coercing nature of capitalistic relations and explaining how the latter might appear as expressions of freedom and equality. Both these problems led him to deepen the role of competition and its relation with capital.

In his work, methodological and ontological issues are strictly related and developed explicitly. The choice of the categories to start with and the method to develop their analysis are consequences of an ontological reasoning: capitalism, like all modes of production, must first of all reproduce itself. Like other modes of production, it is presumably not everlasting. But the fact that it is lasting for centuries suggests that some reproducing mechanisms do in fact exist. The scientific problem is then to discover them and understand how they work. Given the historical nature of the whole mode of production, these reproducing mechanisms have necessarily a historical nature as well.

For ontological reasons, Marx starts from the commodity as elementary category of this mode of production. The production of commodities, he soon notices, depends on the existence of a class of persons in constant need of selling their labour power. Social classes, in this perspective, are not merely theoretical constructs, but essential ontological entities of the capitalist mode of production. The necessity to consider them explicitly is not much of a problem related to their concrete empirical configuration, but is first of all one of internal consistency: an economic model must contain mechanisms that allow the economy reproducing itself.

Competition, in Marx's critique, is the mechanism that regulates this process. More generally, competition regulates the relations among individual capital in the overall process of capital valorisation. In the analysis of these processes, Marx shows that competition produces a number of contradictory tendencies that make the reproduction of the system increasingly problematic and that create the conditions for superseding the capitalist mode of production.

Marx's discussion of competition begins with its historical origins, before the rise of the capitalist mode of production, as a consequence of alienated labour, private property and the market. Capitalism, however, is characterised also by the commodification of labour power, i.e., by the expansion of private property and the market to labour power as well. This is why, in this mode of production, competition takes inevitably a class dimension. With the development of capitalism, capital tends to subsume all human activities and put living labour under its command. In this process, competition imposes its logic over an expanding sphere of social relations and tends to become the coordinating principle of the whole society, the 'external coercive law' of this mode of production, which transforms pre-existing forms of objective and subjective coercion and human nature itself.

Only at this point, can a proper discussion of capitalistic power relations begin. Interpersonal power relations do not develop in a social vacuum, but are embedded in the capitalist system of power. Their essential, necessary, role can be grasped only after having explained the social asymmetries that shape interpersonal relations and the coercive mechanisms that reproduce them. Otherwise, they may appear as mere theoretical possibilities in a power-free context.

At an interpersonal level, the coercive nature of competition manifests itself as an invisible force guiding market participants. No worker is obliged to sell his labour power at the lowest price and no capitalist is obliged to seek the most profitable productions and the less expensive techniques. But if they do not do it, the former does not get the means of subsistence and the latter is put out of the market. Marx's study of a world regulated by competition, therefore, is not an attempt to see how interpersonal relations would be in a system without power and coercion, but a methodological choice intended to isolate the role of this coercive mechanism in the working and reproduction of capitalism.

Bourgeois economists and philosophers have made any effort to develop a conception of competition as the driving force of capitalism towards the common good: Smith, Proudhon, Austrian economists, Walras and post Walrasians have developed different scientific variants of this conception. But they forgot to criticise capital. The result is the celebration of the invisible hand, as a natural mechanism at the service of economic and social progress and a conception of power as its violation. By developing an organic critique of capital, Marx has shown instead that, in fact, this invisible hand only serves the needs of capital. In the capitalist mode of production, the common good is the good of capital and competition simply imposes capital needs over single individuals, social classes and the whole society. In a Marxist conception, the *invisible hand* of competition is nothing but the *armed wing* of capital.

Post Walrasian economics

By contrast, post Walrasian economics and, more generally, neoclassical economics do not start with any ontological reasoning and rarely discuss methodological choices explicitly. In some cases, the a-critical acceptance of methodological individualism is simply a matter of scientific prestige, a condition for being taken seriously in the academic arena. Unlike other methods, indeed, methodological individualism is commonly accepted within mainstream economics and does not need any scientific defence.

The post Walrasian ontology is not built as an attempt to discover the essential categories of capitalism. The conditions of reproducibility of the system are not investigated. Rather, ontology is assumed as an indirect and implicit consequence of methodological choices. Without much philosophical discussion, ontological individualism is assumed as an implicit premise of methodological individualism.

The starting point of the analysis is an abstract model (the Walrasian model), not a historical reality. The problem is not to understand how capitalism works and reproduces itself, but to explain how power relations can be introduced in a general equilibrium framework. Hence the debate on power is basically an exercise in pure logic. These theories can at best solve the problems of the Walrasian model, by means of new assumptions, but cannot explain the nature of power relations in the real history of capitalism.

With these premises, the eventual existence of power relations is sought in the asymmetries between interacting individuals in a given DMC. Human nature and imperfections become *dei ex machina*, universal causes that cannot be explained. Social classes play no essential role in the working of the economy. They can be formalised explicitly – as empirical homogeneous groups of persons – or taken implicit. Yet, they are superfluous add-ons, since the model works even without them.

In the post Walrasian ontology, the nature of power relations can only be found within the interpersonal relation itself. By construction, the latter can have a power content only by introducing imperfections. In this ontology, there is no room for social coercion and power relations can exist only as violations of perfectly competitive interactions. The notion of power incorporates thus the theory of perfect competition as its essential premise and its study becomes little more than an appendix of the perfectly competitive model. From a Marxist perspective, the theoretical contribution of post Walrasian economics is then easily summarised: by starting from a mystified conception of competition, it develops a mystified conception of power.

The bizarre thing is that one of the main impulses to the academic debate on power came indeed from the radical school, whose exponents often affirm to have affinities with Marxism. These authors, however, do not develop Marx's conception and his critique of political economy. Rather, without understanding that the latter applies largely to them as well, they a-critically adopt a neoclassical methodology and then try to obtain conclusions with a Marxist sound.

The idea is that Marx's method is weak and fuzzy and that only a strict neoclassical method can overcome its internal limits. The historical rise of neoclassical economics – an academic reaction against Marxism and its revolutionary implications – is taken as the birth of the universal economic method, to which even Marx should be converted. As a scientist, Marx is worthless. Only some of his non-scientific intuitions might perhaps be saved (for reasons that Marx himself could not understand). This is the consideration of 'radical' neoclassical economists for the founder of scientific socialism. This is the logic of this new 'heterodox' academic fashion: either Marxism becomes a corollary of neoclassical economics or it is condemned to be scientific bullshit ('non-bullshit Marxism' is the self-assigned label of analytical Marxists).

Unfortunately, neoclassical economics cannot be bought *à la carte*. When you buy its method, you buy its implicit ontology and its ideological premises as well. The result is that the same statement – that the capitalist has power over the worker – takes a completely different meaning with respect to Marx's conception.

Within this conception, the only way to demonstrate that economic relations might involve power is to play with assumptions. 'Imperfections' and 'individuals with heterogeneous innate qualities' are the pieces of the game chosen by both neoclassical radicals and their neoliberal opponents, within an implicit ontology based on free contracting and pure circulation. In playing this game, Bowles, Gintis and their post Walrasian colleagues have not found anything better than assuming an asymmetry in favour of the individual worker against the individual capitalist, before the exchange, in order to explain why, after the exchange, the latter has power over the former.

Their story begins with the advantage of the individual worker and finishes with the capitalist having power over him/her. But only because, in the middle, the worker's initial advantage is monetised. The power relation suffered by the worker appears thus to be caused by his/her supposedly favourable position with respect to the capitalist, not the other way round. Reality is so turned upside-down as in the old mystified conception of vulgar economics. Although post Walrasians do not like the notion of exploitation, in these theories to power, the exploited one might eventually be the capitalist, who pays the rent, but surely not the worker who collects it.

But to fully grasp this mystified conception, we must follow the worker the day in which he/she finally gets rid of his/her power relation with the capitalist: the day in which the latter introduces a new machine, which regulates workers' effort, their pace of work and their mode of coordination with each other. This same day, the worker loses the information advantage, the employment rent and perhaps the job. For post Walrasian radicals, however, this is the day of his/her liberation from the capitalist's power. Now, finally, he/she can leave the capitalist without losing anything (having already lost everything, except his/her labour power). This is freedom in post Walrasian economics.

To show that the capitalist has power over the worker, post Walrasians assume that the individual worker is not a member of the class of persons who have nothing to sell except their labour power, but, on the contrary, that he/she is a privileged person within this class, having also something else to sell (his/her information advantages). Workers at the perfectly competitive (subsistence) wage suffer no power relations in this conception. In a complete overturning of Marx's view, here the interpersonal power relation suffered by the individual worker is not caused by his/her participation in an exploited class, but by his/her privileged position within this class. In a nutshell, in this theory, the worker suffers a power relation not because of his/her social weakness, but because of his/her individual strength.

Some radicals might be satisfied with the formal similarities between their results and Marx's critique. Their conception of science and their role in society, however, resemble closely those of 'the vulgar economist [who] does practically no more than translate the singular concepts of the capitalists ... into a seemingly more theoretical and generalized language, and attempt to substantiate the justice of those conceptions' (Marx 1894, ch. 13).

Economists as servants of power

The 1968 movement remains today one of the most advanced radical, revolutionary movement with a worldwide impact. Those people who fought the power in different spheres of social life and in different angles of the globe had in mind a different society: *they wanted everything, they demanded the impossible* as the only way *to be realist*, they were part of a political struggle encompassing the whole society.[3] Feminism, black power, anti-fascism, anti-imperialism, anti-war, anti-nuclearism, anti-prohibitionism, ecologism, homosexuality, peoples self-determination, in the sixties and the seventies, all aspects of social life were object of collective critique and political struggle. In workplaces, in schools and universities, in the streets and in prisons, everywhere institutionalised power was questioned and overtly fought. Strikes, occupations, self-organisation, counter-culture, music, art, drug, sport became all means to react collectively against the forms of oppression and domination of capitalism. Counter-powers developed everywhere, in a common effort to change the material conditions of this class society, discard the coercive nature of bourgeois hegemonic culture and rethink the rules of social interaction.

For the first time in Western societies, a mass student movement played a major role in social struggles, joined the claims of workers and created a fusion with the civil rights movement in a process of radical critique and social emancipation. The student movement disrupted academic equilibria and imposed a radical reaction against mainstream thinking in all social sciences. In the United states, these processes led to the birth of the radical school, an academic project based more on common progressive political goals than on a general method and conception.

The academic debate on power is to a large extent a product of these social and political movements. Forced by the contradictions of society and by overt political struggles, social scientists have been called to take position: on the one hand, those who tried to hide, justify or rationalise the existing forms of power and coercion; on the other, those who criticised them and searched the way to attenuate or supersede them. It is within this historical context that some progressive academicians have developed this curious theoretical exercise, wishing to 'rehabilitate' Marx within mainstream economics.

Like old revisionisms, post Walrasian radicals start by formally declaring sympathy for Marx, but soon after distance themselves from his method and critique. Rather than developing a theoretical conception of power that might give coherence to the collective struggles growing in society, post Walrasians have developed a framework in which power is good for the individual and collective action is only a deplorable form of monopoly. Students and society demanded critical thinking and attacked frontally all institutionalised powers, including academic hierarchies. 'Radical' teachers and researchers answered by developing a theoretical framework in which 1) the greatest worldwide wave of collective struggles appears simply as an irrational, scientifically unfounded, reaction against an only imaginary world of social coercion and 2) the sole rigorous science of power has to do with isolated individuals fighting for themselves.

To affirm this general conception of power, post Walrasian economists have worked hard. They have developed an abstract, universally valid, framework and have applied it to all fields of social interaction, from grocery's shopping to international relations. Radicals, in particular, have pushed this conception very far and have concluded that power relations are practically ubiquitous. Curiously, however, they have never considered that, as scientists, they too are embedded in a community ruled by power relations and which reproduces itself by means of particular rules and mechanisms, whose effect is to shape and select scientific production. In their view – but this is a widely shared opinion even outside the academia – universities are places of critical thinking, scientific autonomy and research freedom, *par excellence*. Scientific rigour and technical skills, not power relations, class interests and cultural homologation, are the keys to academic success. *Voilà*, after a contradictory scientific path, the last contradiction of this academic approach to power, which pretends to be radical: power is everywhere, but in the academy.[4]

Historically, university professors have not been very inclined to criticise the system of power that gives them economic privileges and social recognition. Instead, they have shown high degrees of adaptability to all kinds of economic and political power. When, in 1931, Benito Mussolini imposed the fascist oath in Italian universities, out of more than 1200 academicians, only in twelve refused it (and were thus excluded from their roles).[5] And when today European university teachings and researches are redefined, under the international coordination of the so called 'Bologna process', to meet the needs of international capital restructuring, professors and researchers are again adapting meekly to their new economic and social functions. In market-oriented university systems, then, the role of power relations is not really weaker: apparently, political power is less invasive, but only because universities are already under a tight control of economic power.

Although university systems work and reproduce themselves according to different mechanisms in different countries, they all play a delicate role in scientific and cultural production. Only in the head of the scientist, who does not recognise his social and economic role, can university be conceived as 'free' and science as 'neutral'. Only such a scientist can think that the success of his theory of power has nothing to do with the real power relations existing in society. It is not by chance, however, that the sharpest critique of intellectuals was developed by Gramsci – while he was paying the price of his radical thinking and political coherence in fascist prisons – not by a progressive economist believing in science neutrality.

Gramsci (1929–35) also explained that 'All men are intellectual' since 'There is no human activity from which every form of intellectual participation can be excluded'. His critique, therefore, is not about intellectuals as such, but about the social function of this professional category. In his revolutionary strategy, the problem is to create a 'new stratum of intellectuals', whose mode of being consists in 'active participation in practical life', in social struggles within the masses, in expressing the feelings and the instances of social movements. Only such an intellectual can play a revolutionary role against traditional intellectuals and their intrinsic conservatism.

But, of course, this process does not develop out of class relations, but within them, with open clashes between different class cultures and practices. Without conscious resistance, the interests and values of the ruling classes tend to prevail and to appear as interests and values of the whole society, so that even dominated classes identify their own good with the good of the ruling classes. This why, under the title of the weekly *L'Ordine Nuovo*, co-funded by Gramsci, a slogan reads:

Educate yourself, because we'll need all your intelligence. Agitate yourself, because we'll need all your enthusiasm. Organise yourselves, because we'll need all your strength.

'Cultural hegemony', for Gramsci, is not the *ex post* result of freely competing cultures, but a political strategy on both sides of class struggle.

It is indifferent the good or bad faith of the individual scientist. The rise of post Walrasian economics is part of this hegemonic process, which characterises the neoliberal era. The project itself to force Marx's revolutionary ideas into mainstream economics is a manifestation of the role of cultural hegemony in science as well. Rather than rehabilitating Marx, these projects do in fact exclude his conception from the set of what they define rigorous science. Post Walrasian economists pretend to fly higher than Marx because of their scientific rigour and neutrality. Without understanding that it is only their being part of a hegemonic process that makes them appear as scientifically neutral.

Post Walrasian radicals not only miss the bourgeois nature of their theories but do not even grasp the political role they actually play. In their 'neutral' conception of power, the power of the capitalist over the worker is in the interest of the worker. And the objective need (for capital and for its master, but apparently for its sycophant too) to force the pace, the intensity and the overall effort of the worker, again, is only for the own good of the latter. This is what leftist economists affirmed when Thatcher and Reagan started the neoliberal program.

Although post Walrasians might be convinced that their academic success is only a matter of science, when the mechanisms of academic production and reproduction are put in relation with the social and economic function of the university within the capitalist system, a more linear explanation emerges: the appeal of this approach is not necessarily in its self-proclaimed scientific superiority, but in its ability to incorporate even the most radical critique of capitalism within the more convenient framework of neoliberal culture and politics, thereby depriving it from all its subversive and revolutionary contents.

In 1974, before the development of post Walrasian economics, Bowles wrote an article titled 'Economists as servants of power', in which he discusses the 'immense ... possibilities for socially concerned economists', if only they decide to work with social movements, and criticises 'conventional economists', by dividing them in two groups: the 'Engineers' – 'neo-Keynesian stabilisers' and other economists working 'to "rationalize" production and increase profits for the large corporation' – and the 'Priests', 'neoclassical theorists for the most part', playing a 'less useful, but no less important' ideological role, whose impact is 'to obfuscate the sources of social problems, locating the roots of inequality and hierarchy in the nature of man (preferences) or the state of nature (technology), thereby denying the possibility of a substantially better society'.

It is hard for an economist to choose between these different roles. Only a theory of power based on the spontaneous maximisation of workers' effort, under the principle of economic efficiency, could aspire to have it both ways.

Reorienting the struggle

The conceptions of capitalism as a system of power or as a set of interpersonal relations – governed either by power or by competition – suggest very different approaches to economic research and political struggle.

In the first conception, research and struggle should be oriented at transforming the system, its constraining and conditioning structures and its coercing mechanisms. Association and collective action are the material basis of counter powers and the ways to contrast competition. Social and political struggle is the very danger for capitalist power. Workers' solidarity is the strength of the individual worker and of the entire working class. Their union is the concrete way to transform power relations in the workplace and in society and, more generally, the union of the oppressed is the way to contrast and abolish oppression.

In the second conception, power is an individual problem. The submission to a power relation is an individual choice aiming at receiving privileges from the transacting party. It is an individual strategy that divides, does not unite. Workers' association is only a form of monopoly and counter-power is an empty concept. The whole theoretical framework is little more than a formalisation of the *carrot and stick* approach as an everlasting truth, without even seeing it as a class strategy. The old Julius Caesar's maxim *divide ut regnes* is no longer seen as a tyrannic strategy to gain and maintain power, but as a state of nature to take for granted.

Starting from these general differences, let me conclude by spending some words on two political issues that seem to me crucial in the definition of a strategy of resistance and counteroffensive against the capitalist system of power.

Class struggle

The first political consequence of the post Walrasian approach that I wish to develop regards the end of class struggle: class struggle, in this approach, is simply nonsensical. First, because class relations do not exist in the post

Walrasian ontology. Second, because the notion of struggle is extraneous to this approach.

Of course, social classes can be introduced as statistical aggregates in any microeconomic model, but cannot play any substantial role in this ontology. If Marx and Engels (1848, ch. 1) believed that 'The history of all hitherto existing society is the history of class struggles', post Walrasian economics suggests instead that it is a history of harmonious societies, evolving according to Pareto improvements, giving rise occasionally to some interpersonal power relation.

Even collective action becomes a matter of personal convenience in this approach. To quote again the leaders of radical post Walrasianism, employment rents 'are not only enforcement instruments, they are also prizes to be won or enhanced through collective action. Collusion by one group of workers to exclude others on the basis of racial, gender, or ethnic differences, for example, can increase the employment rents of this group' (Bowles and Gintis 1990, p. 197).

In this framework, workers' union is not in the first instance a tool to resist capital, but a strategy to beat other workers in the struggle for the capitalist's carrot. Collective action is not an emancipatory practice, but a cause of discriminations. Faced with the many overlapping sources of power and coercion flowing from class, racial, gender and ethnic relations, post Walrasians do not even try to disentangle this complex set of social relations and, eventually, suggest how to struggle against this multiform oppression. Instead, they provide a rationalisation of the battle of the have-nots, in which socially discriminated groups find their enemy in other oppressed groups, not in the general cause of their oppression, namely capital.

According to post Walrasian economics, collective bargaining, strikes, occupations and all the practices historically developed in class struggle are irrational behaviours and violations of the common good. It would be clearly exaggerated to blame an academic approach for the real transformations of society. But this is precisely how the direct attacks on wages, centralised bargaining and workers' rights – including the right to struggle – have been imposed in the last decades in most of the globe: not as forms of class struggle against the proletariat, but as technical solutions for the good of everybody.

The obvious corollary of this approach is that only the explicit attempts to resist these processes appear as part of class struggle (and must therefore be condemned), whereas the processes themselves appear as natural and economically efficient. If, in a country, the working week passes from 40 to 45 hours, it is a technical affair, an external condition imposed by international competitiveness, to which everybody should adapt rapidly. If, however workers engage in a struggle to shorten the working week, this is inefficient and will damage the whole country.

The second reason of the disappearance of class struggle from post Walrasian economics is the methodological exclusion of struggles in general. Indeed, in this approach, the system is taken as given and assumed to change automatically to serve at best the wishes of everybody, therefore, the possibility to transform it by means of struggles is both illogical and undesirable.

In the post Walrasian framework, the problem is to define an optimal strategy *within* the existing norms and constraints. But the problem of transforming these norms and constraints cannot be posed. Social asymmetries are not denied, but taken as given, and individual rationality is defined within these social asymmetries, with the obvious result that revolutionary practises – or, simply, attempts to modify the existing asymmetries – appear as irrational. *Given* the existing norms and constraints, this approach suggests thus the individual worker to think for himself/herself, to go to work when his/her colleagues go on strike and, more generally, to divide from his/her comrades and become a special collaborator of the capitalist. This is workers' rationality in post Walrasian economics.

In social struggles, however, the problem is not merely to take advantage of the contingent power relations, but also to transform these relations and lay the foundations for deeper and more advanced struggles in the future. In a perspective of social change, rationality does not imply at all the cowardice of the neoclassical worker, but is defined dynamically, according to a collective project. Even the choice to violate the rules might be perfectly rational if the historical circumstances require it.

A 'class struggle' within the rules is the dream of any conservative. It equals to struggle by ceding on one front in order to advance on another. This kind of 'struggle' only reinforces the existing power balance, it hardly disrupts it. Historically, however, improvements in the economic and social conditions of the working class and, more generally, of all the dispossessed have often been obtained by breaking the existing rules.

Only when the struggling process impedes concretely the working of a system of power, the latter is forced to deeply transform itself, to change its institutionalised rules, to redefine the set of duties and rights of oppressing and oppressed actors. Only when the mechanisms of reproduction of a system of power jam, another world becomes possible. Post Walrasian economics may teach us that these struggles are incompatible with Pareto efficiency. But nobody has ever thought that class societies might be abolished by means of Pareto improvements.

Counter-powers

The second political issue regards the actors that might develop the struggle and subvert the capitalist system of power. In the post Walrasian ontology, as we have seen, power plays no essential role. Liberals and radicals disagree on the empirical spread of imperfections, but they agree that, when empirical contexts resemble the perfect DMC, power is absent. Therefore, power is only a contingency, a possible, but not necessary, category. As a consequence, there is no room for an ontological distinction between powers and counter-powers as essential or inessential entities.

All forms of power have the same nature and the same cause: imperfections. The worker's right to a job is on the same ground of the capitalist's right to fire him/her, the lessee's right to a home has the same dignity of the lessor's right to take back his apartment, people's right to defend their land is equal to the right of a foreign state to militarily occupy it. In this conception, asymmetric rules or direct actions in defence of the weak party of a relation are simply irrational. All rights are the same. And the stronger wins.

The distinction between powers and counter-powers, however, is decisive both in economic research and in political struggle. Conceptually, power emanates directly from the structures and mechanisms of capitalism (and can be reinforced by the conscious action of actors on the dominating side of the system of power); counter-powers arise instead only as conscious responses of the dominated side. This conceptual difference presupposes a critical view on capitalism, in which the structures and mechanisms that govern the system are not power-free but play instead an asymmetric coercive role. To *let things go*, in this system, is not the way towards individual freedom and social recomposition but a strategy that reinforces the forms and degrees of capitalistic power and coercion: when rules are symmetrical and power relations asymmetrical, it is not difficult to predict who will get stronger and who will get weaker.

In many capitalist democracies, the necessity to protect the weak side of power relations is recognised as constitutive element of social interaction. Explicit asymmetrical rules are (or, more correctly, were) often introduced to counter-balance the asymmetric conditions prevailing in society. But when this happens, it is because of the struggles of counter-powers, not thanks to the design of a *super-partes* political philosopher.

An ontological confusion between power and counter-powers serves only the needs of the dominating side of a system of power: it suggests that workers' strikes and capitalists' lockouts are the same thing; it gives the same legitimacy to the *Ku Klux Klan*, wishing to impose white supremacy, and the *Black Panther Party*, struggling for black people self defence; it justifies Israeli soldiers shooting Palestinian people for throwing stones against occupying tanks.

The theoretical and practical separation of powers and counter-powers is the necessary condition to develop a general and coherent strategy to overturn a system of power. Capitalist power is shaped by capitalist exploitation and its real danger comes then from the struggles that transform this class relation. Historically, production stoppages, strikes and pickets, sabotages, boycotts, occupations and workers' self-management, self-reductions and proletarian expropriations have been forms of struggle that have both strengthen proletarian solidarity and weakened capital in its valorisation process. But capitalist power is not limited to the production and circulation processes. It affects all aspects of social life. This opens many possibilities for counter-powers. Capital can be attacked and weakened in the workplace, at school and at the university, in the defence of rights, in the defence of territories, in the safeguard of the planet, in culture, in music and art, in sport, within and outside the law. But all this needs conscious action and organisation.

This is the very challenge in the development of counter-powers. Unlike powers, counter-powers do not develop spontaneously and when they manage to be effective, in this mystified system, they immediately appear as attacks to the sacred rules of free competition. The more counter-powers hit the heart of the capitalist system of power, the more they appear as sources of inefficiencies and violations of the 'universal' values of the bourgeoisie. And, as a consequence, the harder is their social condemnation and political repression. This is why a struggle within a system of power is a much more complex issue than a fight between isolated individuals.

The neoliberal cultural hegemony is today the main obstacle to the development of counter-powers with a real anti-systemic vision. Yet, when a growing part of society has nothing to lose but its chains, counter-powers become a necessity. This is the contradiction of our time: objective coercion increases with the progressive subsumption of society under capital, but 'radical thinking' runs after the myth of competition of mainstream culture and science. The history of capitalism shows that when capital is left free to operate, it tends to subjugate the whole society. But it shows also that anywhere capital imposes its coercive law, society does not follow academic teachings. It self-organises and defends itself from capital.

With this book, I have tried to contribute to give coherence and effectiveness to the many anti-capitalist struggles developing in society, by proposing a general framework for the analysis and transformation of capitalistic power relations. I have also suggested that economists might play an active role in a revolutionary process, if only they started to recognise that even their supposedly neutral science is already part of the struggle, on the conservatory side. I hope that my critique of the neoclassical approach and of its political role will help students and researchers to rethink the role of the social scientist in this society. But I am perfectly aware that only the praxis, not certainly a book, can generate Gramsci's 'revolutionary intellectual'. This is why, if you have had the patient to follow my argument until here, it is time to stop reading.

Notes

1 It is here the case to remember that Stiglitz's efficiency wages theory is more related to exploitation than to efficiency, for the increase in production is not obtained by taking inputs constant, but by increasing the amount of labour extracted by workers' labour power.

2 Within Marxism, Dobb (1973) has discussed the inevitable ideological content of all economic theories. Outside of Marxism, Myrdal (1969) is perhaps the economist that has best illustrated the different levels of value judgements that are introduced in both positive and normative economics. Within neoclassical economics, this problem is considered almost trivial and social desirability is generally identified with Pareto optimality. This equation, however, has been criticised for its philosophical weakness and for the surreptitious introduction of value judgements that it incorporates (Hausman and McPherson 1996). In Gloria-Palermo and Palermo (2005), we discuss the role of value judgements in the normative prescriptions of the two main neoliberal schools, namely Austrian and neoclassical economics.

3 *Vogliamo tutto* (*We want everything*) is the title of a political document about the struggles of 'Potere operaio' within the Italian movement (Balestrini 1974). *Soyons réalistes, demandons l'impossible!* (*Let's be realistic, demand the impossible!*) was one of the most striking slogans of the French movement in May 1968, often attributed to Che Guevara.

4 With the notable exception of Bourdieu (1984), academicians have rarely tried to apply their theories of power to the university system in order to criticise its internal mechanisms and its economic and social functions. I have tried to contribute to this critique by discussing the Italian university system as a system of power in Palermo (2012).

5 The fascist oath was preceded by discriminations against women and was followed, in 1938, by the shame of the 'racial laws'. From exile, professor Colonnetti (1973, p. 54) commented the easygoing reaction of his 'colleagues' by calling it 'prostitution of science'. Finzi (1997) reconstructs the stories of the victims of political and racial discriminations and points out that – except for rare but significant exceptions – the whole academia created a curtain of indifference or even contempt against them, which lasted even after the fall of fascism, fearing that their readmission in role might upset the new power balance within faculties. In Palermo (2011), I discuss the role of academic power in the evolution of the social and economic goals of Italian universities, since national unification.

References

Balestrini, Nanni (1974), *Vogliamo tutto*, Milano, Garzanti.

Bowles, Samuel (1974), Economists as servants of power, *American Economic Review*, vol. 64, n. 2, pp. 129–32.

Bowles, Samuels and Herbert Gintis (1990), Contested exchange: New microfoundations for the political economy of capitalism, *Politics and Society*, vol. 18, n. 2, pp. 165–222.

Bourdieu, Pierre (1984), *Homo academicus*, Paris, Minuit.

Colonnetti, Gustavo (1973), *Pensieri e fatti dell'esilio (18 settembre 1943–7 dicembre 1944)*, Roma, Accademia Nazionale dei Lincei.

Dobb, Maurice (1973), *Theories of value and distribution since Adam Smith: Ideology and economic theory*, Cambridge, Cambridge University Press.

Finzi, Roberto (1997), *L'università italiana e le leggi antiebraiche*, Roma, Editori Riuniti.

Gloria-Palermo, Sandye and Giulio Palermo (2005), Austrian economics and value judgements: A critical comparison with neoclassical economics, *Review of Political Economy*, vol. 17, n. 1, pp. 63–78.

Gramsci, Antonio (1929–35), *Prison notebooks*. Retrieved from www.marxists.org/ archive/gramsci/prison_notebooks/index.htm (accessed 1 March 2016).

Hausman, Daniel and Michael McPherson (1996), *Economic analysis and moral philosophy*, Cambridge, Cambridge University Press.

Marx, Karl (1894), *Capital: Critique of political economy, vol, 3, The process of capitalist production as a whole*. Retrieved from www.marxists.org/archive/ marx/works/1894-c3/index.htm (accessed 1 March 2016).

Marx, Karl and Frederick Engels (1848), *The communist manifesto*. Retrieved from www.marxists.org/archive/marx/works/1848/communist-manifesto/index.htm (accessed 1 March 2016).

Myrdal, Gunnar (1969), *Objectivity in social research*, New York, Pantheon books.

Palermo, Giulio (2011), *L'università dei baroni: Centocinquant'anni di storia tra cooptazione, contestazione e mercificazione*, Milano, Punto Rosso.

——(2012), *Baroni e portaborse: I rapporti di potere nell'università*, Roma, Editori International Riuniti.

Stiglitz, Joseph (1993), Post Walrasian and post Marxian economics, *Journal of Economic Perspectives*, vol. 7, n. 1, pp. 109–14.

Index

Printed in the United States
by Baker & Taylor Publisher Services

Printed in the United States
by Baker & Taylor Publisher Services